What You Need to Know About Mary

(But Were Never Taught)

Scott L. Smith

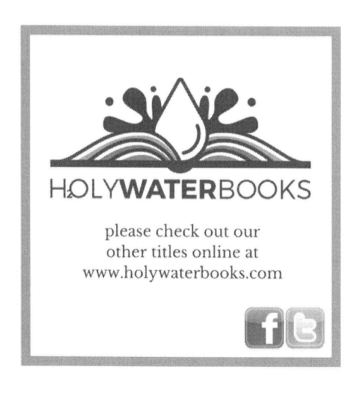

HOLY**WATER**BOOKS

please check out our
other titles online at
www.holywaterbooks.com

Table of Contents

PART ONE:
The New Eve

Chapter 1:
The Greatest
Verse in the Bible

I'm going to tell you the greatest verse in all of Scripture. You might be saying, how could he even say that? How could there be a "greatest" verse – isn't that supremely subjective? Just a matter of opinion? I don't think so.

In one verse, God makes known His entire plan of salvation, his entire plan for all of human history. Not only that, he does this *at the very beginning* of human history. This one verse demonstrates that God is the Lord of all history.

Everybody has their favorite Bible verse, right? I know there are a number of people who would claim John 3:16 as their favorite: "For God so loved the world that he gave his only Son, that whoever believes in Him should not perish but have eternal life." It's hard to compete with that one, right? Or, Psalm 23, "The Lord is my shepherd, I shall not want." Surely, the greatest verse in Scripture *must* be between those two, right? No, I don't think so.

Jesus Christ is the Word of God incarnated as a human person. Christ is, Himself, the sum total of Scripture and much,

much more, besides. I imagine that every time Jesus spoke, all of eternity echoed in his voice. You could and *still can* hear all of Scripture in every word that comes from Jesus's mouth. So, then, does the entirety of the Word ever appear in a single verse?

The early days of the Christian Church, those first few centuries after Christ, have been called the Age of Miracles. These were the years Saints Peter and Paul and the first few generations of Apostles were traveling around the Roman world, even the entire world, and converting the masses. In those days, the primary modes of credibility of Jesus' Church were (1) prophesy and (2) miracles.

There is one verse that, by itself, shows the Age of Miracles is not for a time, but for all time. This one verse is miracle and prophesy *combined*.

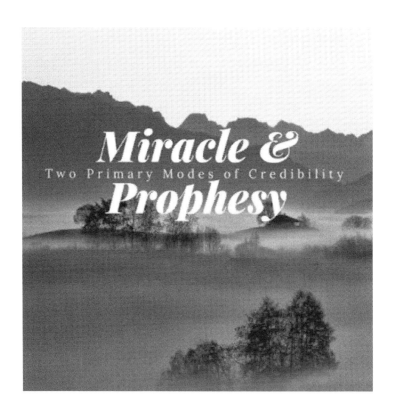

Miracle & Prophesy

Two Primary Modes of Credibility

How could one verse be the greatest in all of Scripture? Only if that one verse was the greatest prophesy of the greatest miracles of all time. This one verse would need to contain *all of the Gospel* message in itself. Not only that, this one verse would need to have told the entire Gospel story long before it even happened. How long? Would a hundred years be enough? Five hundred? How about fifteen hundred years? Or more? What if this one verse was a part of the oldest story known to man?

Only a verse which could do all those things could rightfully be called the greatest verse in all of Scripture. And this verse does.

Not only that, to be called the greatest, this one verse must be a very powerful tool for evangelization. If it contains within itself the two primary modes of credibility, namely prophesy and miracle, this one verse would be very powerful indeed. The mere existence of this verse, if it is the greatest in all of Scripture, ought to generate conversion after conversion.

But how could one verse be and do so much? Because this one verse is the Word of God, who was made flesh within the Virgin. All of Scripture is the Word of God, but this one verse is God's own Word on the subject. In this one verse, God, Himself, speaks the Word, the Gospel itself, to all mankind through our first parents. When God spoke this one particular word it was the Word, Himself, in embryonic form. When God spoke this Word, both simultaneously and thousands of years into the future, the Immaculate Virgin was conceived *and* she conceived in her womb.

Yes! When God spoke this Word at the dawn of history to our first parents, Adam and Eve, our new parents, Jesus and Mary, were conceived. This one Word of God – ancient to us, but not to "He Who Is" – was both the conception of the Immaculate Virgin and the conception of Christ within her womb.

Lastly, this one verse is the greatest of all because it is the very Word of God that brought about "The Greatest Story Ever Told", the Gospel. God never just prophesies. As great as Isaiah, Jeremiah, and Daniel were, God is no mere prophet.

God brings about what He prophesies. God writes history with His Word.

So, what were these words that gave the Word to Man?

The answer is in the next chapter.

Chapter 2:
The First
Prophesy in
Human History

What is the *very* **first prophesy** in human history? What or *who* is it about? As you might imagine, it's probably be pretty important.

This single verse, Genesis 3:15, is called the "Proto-evangelium," which means "First Gospel." This one verse is the first mention of the Gospel in Scripture, and it occurs right after the Fall of Adam and Eve. Not only that, it's an encapsulation -- the "seed" -- of the entire Gospel. There is a summary of the Gospel hidden right here in this short verse. This means that God knew His plan to redeem all mankind *from the very beginning,* and said so.

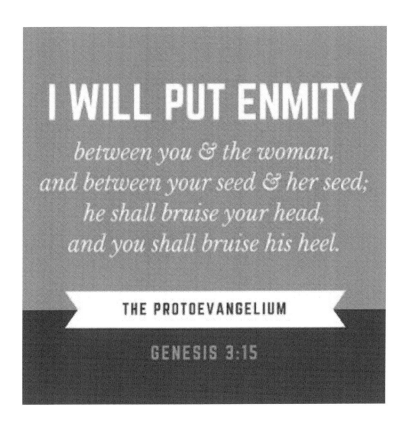

I WILL PUT ENMITY

*between you & the woman,
and between your seed & her seed;
he shall bruise your head,
and you shall bruise his heel.*

THE PROTOEVANGELIUM

GENESIS 3:15

Not only does Genesis 3:15 contain prophesies of Christ, it also provides three distinct prophesies of the Blessed Virgin Mary *that every Catholic should know.*

Take a second to think about that. This was written thousands of years before Mary's birth. How inexpressibly amazing is it that this verse would contain prophesies of her life? Also, how amazing is that that God would hinge all history on the life of a Nazarene peasant girl and her willingness to say yes? What a miracle! As Mary did, just ponder that in the silence of your heart.

Where does this verse appear in Scripture? This verse immediately follows the fall of Adam and Eve after their temptation by the serpent. God addresses each one in turn -- the serpent, Eve, and Adam (as well as the New Eve and the New Adam). Gen 3:15 is actually part of God's address to the serpent.

There is quite a lot happening in these four lines. Let's break it down, piece by piece, prophesy by prophesy:

Who's Who in This Passage?

We need to identify our cast of characters. Who is "I", "you/her", "the woman", "your", "he/his", etc.? All these pronouns can get tricky.

To explain Who's Who, I've made the following infographic:

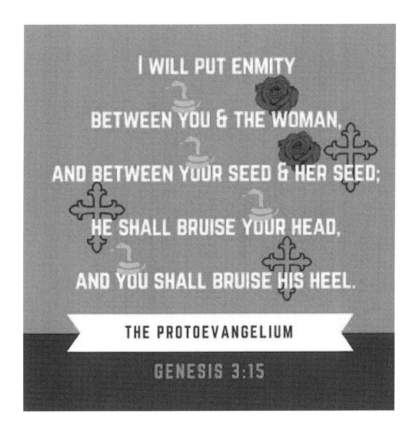

I WILL PUT ENMITY BETWEEN YOU & THE WOMAN, AND BETWEEN YOUR SEED & HER SEED; HE SHALL BRUISE YOUR HEAD, AND YOU SHALL BRUISE HIS HEEL.

THE PROTOEVANGELIUM

GENESIS 3:15

The coiled serpent is the serpent and the seed of the serpent. The rose is "the woman". The cross is Jesus, the "seed" of the woman.

Or, if plain text is clearer to you, I've inserted names into the verse below and alongside the pronouns:

> I [God] will put enmity between you [the serpent] and the woman [Mary], and
> between your [the serpent's] seed and her [Mary's] seed;
> he [Jesus] shall bruise your [the serpent's] head,
> and you [the serpent] shall bruise his [Jesus'] heel.

God is speaking to Eve, Adam, and the serpent, but "the woman" is not Eve. *It is Mary.* Trust me on this for now, this part will be explained more fully below in the "Immaculate Conception" section. For now, notice that God says He "*will* put emnity", so "the woman" will be a future woman, not Eve. Remember, also, that Jesus refers to his mother as "woman" in the New Testament, specifically at the Wedding in Cana.

For more on the Wedding in Cana, check out the chapter later on in the book entitled, "The Hidden Throne & the Blessed Mother" and "What's Really Happening at the Wedding in Cana."

Who is the serpent? Your gut probably tells you that the serpent is none other than Satan, himself. This is correct. Nevertheless, Scripture confirms this interpretation. Revelation 12 depicts a scene between a "woman" and the "dragon", and refers to the dragon as "that ancient serpent" (Rev 12:9). And *yes,* Revelation speaking of the "woman" and the "serpent" together is extremely significant. Revelation 12 is, in many ways, the sister chapter to Genesis 3, the former fulfills the later.

Who is the serpent's seed? There are multiple interpretations here. The two most common understandings are either (1) the anti-Christ or (2) those who have made covenant with Satan, which could be Cain and his descendants or basically any evil or sinful person. Ultimately, the serpent's seed are those who stand in opposition to the Messiah.

Where is Mary in all this? There are actually three prophesies of Mary in this short verse:

Prophesy #1: The Immaculate Conception

What about that strange word, "enmity". Enmity, according to Google, means "the state or feeling of being actively opposed or hostile to someone or something." We might think of "enmity" as the opposite of "amity" or "amicable".

God says He "*will* put emnity between [the serpent] and [the woman]." Clearly, "the woman" cannot be Eve, because she has already succumbed to serpent's wiles and temptations. She gave into the serpent by eating of the fruit of the Tree of Knowledge. There is no longer enmity or conflict between Eve and the serpent, because, unfortunately, they are allies according to the wages of sin. With her openness to sin, Eve is no longer opposed to Satan.

But! There "will" come "the woman" who will be in conflict with Satan. She will be opposed to Satan from the moment of her conception. She will have been conceived without sin. The Original Sin of Adam and Eve will hold no sway over this woman. This woman is, of course, Immaculate Mary.

Saint Irenaeus states the knot tied by Eve's disobedience was undone by the New Eve's, Mary's, obedience.[1] The "*Ave* Maria" reverses the sin of "Eva" ("Ave" spelled backwards). Mary's YES to God that she will bear the Christ child is an act of open hostility to Satan. Mary's YES is an act of war, i.e. enmity.

---

[1] Saint Irenaeus of Lyons, *Against Heresies*, Book III, Chapter 22, Par. 4.

Figure 1: Image of the Virgin Mary, the New Eve, lifting the first Eve up from her "fallen" state.

Prophesy #2: The Virgin Birth

The words "virgin" or "birth" are not mentioned in the above verse, so how can the Protoevangelium possibly foretell the birth of the Messiah by a virgin? It's all in just two words: "her seed", meaning Mary's seed.

Okay, but how does *that* mean virgin birth?

Everywhere else in Scripture, a child is referred to as *his father's* seed. Jesus is called the "seed of David," for example, because his great-great-great-(...)-grandfather was King David. Or, take Jeremiah 33:26, in which the whole nation of Israel is referred to as the "seed of Jacob."

Referring to Jesus as *his mother's* seed, i.e. "her seed", means the child will have *no biological father*. In other words, a "virgin birth." There was no physical seed of man at Jesus' conception. Thus, it is foretold that the Messiah would be born of a virgin.

Prophesy #3: Defeat of Satan by the Messiah

The next prophesy is that the son of "the woman", i.e. Mary's son, will bruise the head of the seed of "the serpent." In doing so, however, Mary's son will also be wounded in the heel.

What does all this mean? Basically, it means that Jesus will defeat Satan, but in doing so, Jesus will die. That's always the price of the serpent's bite. This is a prophesy, therefore, of Christ's passion, death, and ultimate victory.

But it goes even deeper than this. Can you think of the exact moment when Jesus strikes at the serpent's head or, more specifically, the serpent's *skull*?

Ask yourself, *where* is Jesus crucified? The hill's name is Golgotha, the place of the SKULL. Jesus' cross, the site of his victory over Satan, literally strikes a skull. Again, this is why there is typically a skull depicted at the foot [read: heel] of the cross. Another level of cool: there's a legend that Golgotha was so-named because it was where Adam was buried.[2]

---

[2] According to the New Advent Catholic Encyclopedia, under the entry "Mount Calvary," there was a tradition current among the Jews that the skull of Adam, after having been confided by Noah to his son Shem, and by the latter to Melchisedech, was finally deposited at the place called, for that reason, Golgotha. The Talmudists and the Fathers of the Church were aware of this tradition, and it survives in the skulls and bones placed at the foot of the crucifix. The Evangelists are not opposed to it, inasmuch as they speak of one and not of many skulls. (Luke, Mark, John, loc. cit.)

This is why Mary and Jesus are often depicted as crushing a serpent under their heels. But why Mary, you might ask. The word for "he" in "he shall bruise [the serpent's] head" can be translated as either "he" or "she". St. Jerome in the Vulgate translation of the Bible actually uses the female pronoun instead of "he".[3] This makes sense. Simeon prophesied of

---

[3] Father John Echert, "Q&A Genesis 3:15," Nov. 10, 2003: While most modern translations render the text of Genesis with the masculine pronoun signifying Christ (in accord with the original Hebrew word for "offspring"), the ancient Latin Vulgate of St. Jerome and various writings of the early Church Fathers reveal the belief of the Church that Mary also participates in the crushing of Satan and so rendered the pronoun in the feminine. As such, just as Jesus is the New Adam who reversed the sin of the original Adam by His absolute obedience to God the Father, so too Mary is the New Eve by the absolute conformity of her will to that of God, as manifested first in her acceptance of the Incarnation. And her role as the Mother of humanity—the New Eve--in the order of grace is manifested in the Gospel of St. John, in the scene beside the Cross of the Lord: 19:26-27 When Jesus saw his mother, and the disciple whom he loved standing near, he said to his mother, "Woman, behold, your son!" Then he said to the dis-

Mary that "a sword will pierce through your own soul also" (Luke 2:35).

Prophesy as Proof

Isn't that amazing? All of these prophesies are contained in just one verse. Not only that, it's the very first prophesy in human history, found at the beginning of the Bible and written thousands of years before Mary's conception. Not only is prophecy proof of the power of God, Genesis 3:15 is scriptural proof for the Catholic teaching of the Immaculate Conception. Every Catholic should know about this, right?

Prophesies like this should help fortify the faith of all Catholics. Moreover, the primary modes of credibility of the early Church were miracles and prophesy. That is, the early Christians convinced people of the truth of their faith by performing miracles in Jesus' name and pointing to the ancient prophesies fulfilled by Christ (and His Mother).

What was true for the early Christians is true for us *today*. This is prime material for evangelization. All of us need to

---

ciple, "Behold, your mother!" And from that hour the disciple took her to his own home.

spread word of this proof of God's supernatural power in and over history.

Part Two:
The New Ark

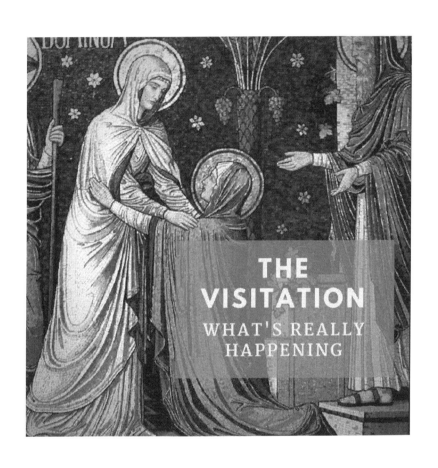

THE
VISITATION
WHAT'S REALLY
HAPPENING

Chapter 1:
What's Really Happening at the Visitation

Mary's visit to Elizabeth was no ordinary family visit. Why does the baby leap in Elizabeth's womb? What other historical event happened in Saint Elizabeth's neighborhood? And what does King David have to do with all this?

There are several details to this Gospel passage that are very subtle. However, once you see them, it becomes clear that the evangelist is intentionally drawing parallels between two passages in Scripture. Luke is referencing a scene in the Old

Testament found at 2 Samuel 6: 2, 5-16, 23, reproduced with emphasis below:

> (2) And **David arose and went** with all the people who were with him from Ba'ale-judah, to bring up from there the ark of God, which is called by the name of the Lord of hosts who sits enthroned on the cherubim ... (5) And David and all the house of Israel were making merry before the Lord with all their might, with songs and lyres and harps and tambourines and castanets and cymbals. (6) And when they came to the threshing floor of Nacon, **Uzzah put out his hand to the ark of God** and took hold of it, for the oxen stumbled. (7) And the anger of the Lord was kindled against Uzzah; and God **smote him there because he put forth his hand to the ark**; and he died there beside the ark of God. (8) And David was angry because the Lord had broken forth upon Uzzah; and that place is called Pe'rez-uz'zah, to this day.

Why did God smite Uzzah? Remember poor Uzzah, but we will be talking about him at the end of this chapter and the beginning of the next one. Back to 2 Samuel 6:

> (9) And David was afraid of the Lord that day; and he said, **"How can the ark of the Lord come to me?"** (10) So David was not willing to take the ark of the Lord into the city of David; but David took it aside to the house of O'bed-e'dom the Gittite. (11) And the ark of the Lord remained in the house of O'bed-e'dom the Gittite **three months**; and the Lord blessed O'bed-e'dom and all his household.

(12) And it was told King David, "The Lord has **blessed the household** of O'bed-e'dom and all that belongs to him, because of the ark of God." So David went and brought up the ark of God from the house of O'bed-e'dom to the city of David with rejoicing; (13) and when those who bore the ark of the Lord had gone six paces, he sacrificed an ox and a fatling. (14) And David **danced before the Lord with all his might**; and David was girded with a linen ephod. (15) So David and all the house of Israel brought up the ark of the Lord with shouting, and with the sound of the horn.

(16) As the ark of the Lord came into the city of David, Michal the daughter of Saul looked out of the window, and saw **King David leaping and dancing before the Lord**; and she despised him in her heart ... (22) And Michal the daughter of Saul had no child **[until] the day of her death**.

Now re-read Luke's account of the Visitation at Luke 1:39-45, 56. Do you notice any similarities?

In those days **Mary arose and went** with haste into **the hill country, to a city of Judah**, and she entered the house of Zechari'ah and greeted Elizabeth. And when Elizabeth heard the greeting of Mary, **the babe leaped in her womb**; and Elizabeth was filled with the Holy Spirit and she **exclaimed** with a loud cry, "Blessed are you among women, and blessed is the fruit of your womb! **And why is this granted me, that the mother of my Lord should come to me?** For behold, when the voice of your greeting came to my ears, the babe in my womb **leaped for joy**. And blessed is she who believed that there would be a fulfillment of what was spoken to her from the Lord." [Mary sings her *Magnificat*] ... And Mary remained with her about **three months**, and returned to her home.

Did you notice anything? What stood out? Some of this might seem obvious. Some of it may be veiled. Let's go through the connections one-by-one:

MARY IS THE NEW ARK

"And why is this granted me, that the mother of my Lord should come to me?"

Elizabeth says this to Mary, but what does David say at 2 Samuel 6:9? "How can **the ark** of the Lord come to me?" Elizabeth just replaces "the mother" for "the ark". Elizabeth is quoting King David when she announces Mary's arrival. Luke is plainly equating the "ark of the Lord" and the "mother of my Lord."

The Babe "Leaped for Joy"

Where could there possibly be a connection here, right? There's no baby at all described in 2 Samuel 6. But there were people "leaping" in both passages: King David was "**leap-**

ing and dancing before the Lord". Therefore, both King David the and the unborn John the Baptist were leaping before the Ark.

Not only that, there were both naked! Michal, the one who is struck barren, rebukes David at 2 Samuel 6:20: "How the king of Israel honored himself today, uncovering himself today before the eyes of his servants' maids, as one of the vulgar fellows shamelessly uncovers himself!" Michal reveals that David was "uncovered" in public.

"Three Months"

Did you notice the amount of time that the Ark of the Lord remained at the house of Obed-edom? It was "three months" (verse 11). And how long did Mary, the New Ark, remain at the house of Elizabeth? Again, *three months*! Check out verse 56.

"Arose and Went" & "The Hill Country of Judah"

First off, the first few words of both passages are repeated: David "arose and went" and Mary, too, "arose and went". These are all tags used by Luke to connect the passages. Moreover, David was coming from "Ba'ale-**judah**" and Mary was headed "in haste" into "the hill country, to a city of **Judah**." Both were in the lands of Judah!

Elizabeth lived in the "hill country" of Judah. But "what has this to do" with King David and the Ark? Where is the Ark headed in 2 Samuel 6? In this chapter, the Ark travels from Abinadab in Gibeah to the house of Obededom the Gittite[4] and then to the "City of David." *So where were all these locations?*

Before the Ark arrived at the house of Obed-edom, Uzzah made his fateful mistake (more on why this was a mistake below). The place where he touched the Ark and was smote dead by God is called "Perez-Uzzah to this day" according to 2 Samuel 6:8. While "to this day" was quite a long time ago, the place is still known.

---

[4] Gath was one of the five royal cities of the Philistines. Gath was also famous as the birthplace or residence of Goliath (1 Samuel 17:4). David fled from Saul to Achish, king of Gath (1 Samuel 21:10; 27:2-4; Psalms 56), and his connection with it will account for the words in 2 Samuel 1:20. It was afterwards conquered by David (2 Samuel 8:1). It occupied a strong position on the borders of Judah and Philistia (1 Samuel 21:10; 1 Chronicles 18:1). Its site has been identified with the hill called Tell esSafieh, which rises 695 feet above the plain on its east edge. The Crusaders built the castle of Alba Specula here in the Middle Ages. It is noticed on monuments about B.C. 1500. Interestingly, "Gath" translates as "wine vat," which may have certain typological and specifically Eucharistic meaning. For more information, see Gath and Tell es-Safi.

After Uzzah's mistake, David hesitated in bringing the Ark into the "City of David." The "City of David" is Jerusalem, and David and his group were almost there.

All of these places - Baale-Judah, the "threshing floor of Nacon," Perez-Uzzah, and the house of Obed-edom - are all within a couple miles of each other. These are all near the ancient city of Kirjath-jearim, which is northwest of Jerusalem.[5]

So if Kirjath-jearim is where the events of 2 Samuel 6 took place, *where was the home of Zechariah and Elizabeth?*

Zechariah and Elizabeth's home is well known. It is near Ein Karem. Zechariah had two homes, one in the valley and a summer home higher up on the hillside, where it was cooler. The home in the valley is the site of the Church of the Nativity of John the Baptist. The home up on the hillside is the site of the Church of the Visitation.

---

[5] The ark was brought to this place (1 Samuel 7:1, 2) from Beth-shemesh and put in charge of Abinadab, a Levite. Here it remained till it was removed by David to Jerusalem (2 Samuel 6:2, 3, 12; 1 Chronicles 15:1-29; compare Psalms 132). It was also called Baalah (Joshua 15:9) and Kirjath-baal. It has been usually identified with Kuriet el-'Enab (i.e., "city of grapes"), among the hills, about 8 miles northeast of 'Ain Shems (i.e., Beth-shemesh). The opinion, however, that it is to be identified with 'Erma, 4 miles east of 'Ain Shems, on the edge of the valley of Sorek, seems to be better supported.

Figure 2: Church of the Visitation and Gorny Monastery, Ein Karem, near Jerusalem

How far apart do you think the site of the Visitation is from the house of Obed-edom, near Kirjath-jearim? Would it surprise you to learn that they are only about 3-4 miles apart as the crow flies?

So not only did these two events both happen in the "hill country of Judah" - both happened *in the same neighborhood!*

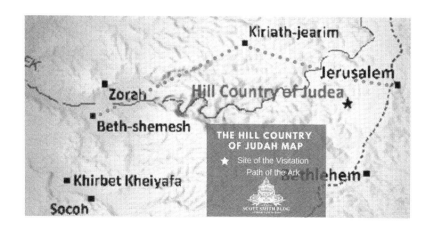

The Hill Country of Judah Map. Site of the Visitation. Path of the Ark.

"Exclaimed"

At Luke 1:42, Elizabeth bursts out with an exuberant cry. Elizabeth "**exclaimed** with a loud cry, 'Blessed are you among women, and blessed is the fruit of your womb!'" She is basically the first human to pray the "Hail Mary!" Remember that you are repeating the words of Elizabeth and the Angel Gabriel when we pray this ancient prayer.

The particular expression used for "exclaim" is very interesting. It is rarely used in the Bible and only ever in a very specific context. This is actually the only time it is found at all in the New Testament.

Every time this word is used in the Old Testament, it refers to the music of the Levitical singers and musicians that accompanied processions of the Ark of the Covenant. It described the "exultant" sound of instruments as the Ark processed into Jerusalem with King David (1 Chronicles 15:28) and into the Temple with King Solomon (2 Chronicles 5:13).

In 2 Samuel 6, the processions of the Ark are also accompanied by music, instruments, and shouting: (verse 5) "And David and all the house of Israel were making merry before the Lord with all their might, with songs and lyres and harps and tambourines and castanets and cymbals"; and (verse 15) "So David and all the house of Israel brought up the ark of the Lord with shouting, and with the sound of the horn."

In summary, when Elizabeth "exlaims" before Mary, she is singing as the New Ark is processing into her home, just as the Levites did at the processions of the original Ark. *And*, there's one more thing. Elizabeth was a Levite!

"Overshadow"

Just as the expression for "exclaim" found in the Visitation is reserved for a certain context in Scripture, so, too, is the word "overshadow." The verse containing "overshadow" occurs a little bit earlier in the Gospel of Luke. It is found at the Annunciation.

If you will recall, the Angel Gabriel said to Mary at Luke 1:35, "The Holy Spirit will come upon you, and the power of the Most High will **overshadow** you."

Like "exclaim," the particular expression for "overshadow" occurs no place else in the New Testament or even Scripture, except at Exodus 40:34-35:

> Then the cloud covered the meeting tent, and the glory of the LORD filled the Tabernacle. Moses could not enter the meeting tent, because the cloud **settled down upon** it and the glory of the LORD filled the Tabernacle.

What was the principal object found within the Tabernacle? *The Ark of the Covenant.*

Luke, therefore, is referencing the way the Spirit of God came upon the Ark as the Glory Cloud (Hb. *shekinah*) to describe the way the Spirit of God will come to the Virgin Mary, the New Ark. Amazing!

Here are some additional insights on Mary provided by 2 Samuel 6:

PERPETUAL VIRGINITY OF MARY
The Curious Incident with Uzzah

So why did God strike Uzzah dead? That seems right out of left field. All Uzzah did was try to stop the Ark from falling off the cart, right?

Figure 3: The Chastisement of Uzzah by James Tissot

Not quite. God's original command was for the *priests*, specifically the Levitical priests, to carry the Ark using the golden poles and rings provided at Exodus 25. Uzzah and his brother were not priests, and the oxen pulling the cart were *certainly* not priests. On top of this irreverence, Numbers

4:15 specifically forbade the Kohathites, such as Uzzah, from touching the Ark and "the holy things, or they will die." God *always* remembers his promises.

But what might this scene say about Mary? If merely touching the original Ark could mean death, what would happen if a mortal man touched, let alone *conceived* with, the Virgin Mary, the spouse of the Holy Spirit? This scene with Uzzah, therefore, provides typological proof for the dogma of the Perpetual Virginity of Mary.

Now, think about how the Virgin Mary was "carried". When do we see Mary being carried? Presumably, she walks on foot to the home of Elizabeth, but there's an extremely iconic moment when Mary is carried. I think you know what I'm getting at … the road to Bethlehem. The Christmas journey!

SIDENOTE: "Until the Day of Her Death"

Here's one more note from 2 Samuel 6 on the Perpetual Virginity of Mary, and then we will return to the Christmas story in the next chapter.

For the hate she bore in her heart for King David, Michal was struck barren, not unlike Uzzah being struck down dead. Elizabeth, too, was believed to be barren, which again connects 2 Samuel 6 to Luke 1.

But there's more! One of the verses most frequently cited to disprove the Perpetual Virginity of Mary is Matthew 1:24-25:

> When Joseph woke from sleep, he did as the angel of the Lord commanded him; he took his wife, but knew her not **until** she had borne a son ...

"See?? Mary was only a virgin until she gave birth to Jesus, and not after!" That's what people will say. Not quite. It's the "and not after" part that is a false assumption. The word "until" when used in Scripture does not mean what it means in every day American English.

How do we know? Compare the "until" in Matthew 1:24-25 with the "until" in 2 Samuel 6:22, "And Michal the daughter of Saul had no child [until] the day of her death."

Does this mean Michal, who was struck barren by God, gave birth to children *after her death*? Absolutely not. In the same way, Joseph is not assumed to have "known" Mary, in the Biblical sense, following Jesus' birth.

Chapter 2:
The New Ark and Christmas

Mary being the Ark of the New Covenant will completely change the way you understand the Christmas story. Hopefully, after reading this chapter you will see Mary and Joseph's journey to Bethlehem in a completely different light, even the light of the Star of Bethlehem, itself.

Why does Mary Travel on a Donkey to Bethlehem?

This is one of the most iconic scenes in human history. It is at the core of the Christmas story. Joseph is walking on foot and leading the donkey. Mary, fully pregnant, is traveling on the donkey's back.

Why?

Have you ever wondered if there was a hidden meaning behind simple scene? There is.

The answer begins with the curious incident with Uzzah that was described in the last chapter. Uzzah was killed just for just touching the Ark of the Covenant. Why?

Why Was a Man Killed for Touching the Ark of the Covenant?

In the last chapter, we talked about the curious incident of Uzzah being struck dead for touching the old Ark of the Covenant. This occurred at 2 Samuel 6. Here again are the specific verses:

(6) And when they came to the threshing floor of Nacon, **Uzzah put out his hand to the ark of God** and took hold of it, for the oxen stumbled. (7) And the anger of the Lord was kindled against Uzzah; and God **smote him there because he put forth his hand to the ark**; and he died there beside the ark of God. (8) And David was angry because the Lord had broken forth upon Uzzah; and that place is called Pe'rez-uz'zah, to this day.

The reason for God's smiting of Uzzah was that he "put forth his hand to the Ark". Uzzah had some other things going against him. There's more on that in the last chapter.

Here's the bottom line ...

Figure 4: Adorazione dei Magi by Gentile da Fabriano (middle section)

The bottom line was this: Only the priests were allowed to carry the Ark of the New Covenant.

The Ark was not supposed to be carried on a cart, pulled by oxen. Why? Well, would you like to be downwind of a team of oxen? Is that a fitting place for the golden box which carried the presence of God, Himself? No.

Also, the Ark was definitely not supposed to be touched by non-priests, like Uzzah. The Ark was never supposed to be in situation in which it could tumble off a cart, requiring someone like Uzzah to "put forth his hand."

Now, compare the travels of the Old Ark through Israel on an ox cart to the travels of the New Ark, the Virgin Mary. Any similarities?

Saint Joseph Carries the New Ark

Saint Joseph, therefore, is serving in the role of priest and carrying the Ark of the New Covenant on the back of a donkey. Joseph, as you will remember, is also a descendent of King David. It is fitting, then, that Joseph should accompany the Ark of the *New* Covenant, just as his forebear traveled with the Ark of the *Old* Covenant.

That's why Mary travels on the back of a donkey.

There's more. What about Bethlehem? Was there perhaps a notable journey of David and the Old Ark to Bethlehem?

Absolutely.

Here are a few verses of King David singing of the Old Ark's journey to Bethlehem from Psalm 132, verses 1-7:

Remember, O Lord, in David's favor,
all the hardships he endured;
how he swore to the Lord
and vowed to the Mighty One of Jacob,
"I will not enter my house
or get into my bed;
I will not give sleep to my eyes
or slumber to my eyelids,
until I find a place for the Lord,
a dwelling place for the Mighty One of Jacob."
Lo, we heard of it in **Eph'rathah**,
we found it in the **fields of Ja'ar**.
"Let us go to his dwelling place;
let us worship at his footstool!"

Wait, you might be saying, where's the mention of Bethlehem? In the time of King David, Bethlehem was known as Eph'rathah, or it is elsewhere named in the Psalms "Ephratah-Bethlehem".[67]

---

6 Biblical scholar Joseph Addison Alexander argues for this understanding: "The only explanation, equally agreeable to usage and the context, is that which makes Ephratah the ancient name of Bethlehem (Genesis 48:7), here mentioned as the place where David spent his youth, and where he used to hear of the ark, although he never saw it till long afterwards, when he found it in the fields of the wood, in the neighbourhood of Kirjathjearim, which name means Forest town, or City of the Woods. Compare 1 Samuel 7:1 with 2 Samuel 6:3-4."

7 Another Biblical scholar, Christopher Wordsworth, states the following: "The Psalmist says, that David himself, even when a youth in Bethle-

Also, what's David mean when he says "I will not enter my house or get into my bed ... until I find a place for the Lord, a dwelling place for the Mighty One of Jacob"? In short, it means that the Old Ark will be in want of a dwelling place or a roof over its head. More on that in a moment ...

Lastly, there's a great amount of humility contained in this comparison. This Ark of God, which traveled through Israel with King David, himself, and which was carried before all of Israel's victorious armies, is now a simple woman, on a the back of a plain donkey, being led by a carpenter.

We should be struck by the majesty contained in such a simple caravan.

But there's still more. This also tells us something about the Perpetual Virginity of Mary.

Mary & Joseph: No Ordinary Marriage

Remember, this is no ordinary marriage between Mary and Joseph. Joseph never *physically* consummates the marriage covenant with Mary. The Holy Spirit enters Mary's womb, but never mortal man. Mary's womb is the birthplace of God. It is

---

hem Ephratah, heard of the sojourn of the ark in Kirjathjearim, and that it was a fond dream of David's boyhood to be permitted to bring up the ark to some settled habitation, which he desired to find (Psalms 132:5)."

the new Holy of Holies. No mortal man is permitted there, except the high priest, namely Jesus. It is the most sacred of sacred grounds.

This is why Uzzah was smote for touching the old Ark of the Covenant. Uzzah wasn't just trespassing on sacred ground. It was as if he had violated the Ark's virginity.

Joseph does not make the mistake of Uzzah! Joseph has no children by Mary. Mary *remains* a virgin.

Vow of Virginity

In fact, Mary indicates that she has taken a perpetual vow of virginity. The Douay-Rheims translation of the Bible gives us the following for at Luke 1:34: "And Mary said to the angel: 'How shall this be done, because **I know not man?**'"

"I know not man" is the literal translation from the Greek text. Other translations try "because I am a virgin" or "because I know not *a* man," but these alternatives don't quite cut the mustard.

Mary's question to the angel makes no sense unless Mary had professed a vow of virginity.

Just a few verses back at verse 27, we are told that Mary and Joseph are already "espoused". Mary and Joseph already have what would be akin to a ratified marriage in Jewish culture. They were *married*. Joseph would have had the right to the marriage bed.

How can we account then for Mary's confusion? Mary did not say simply: "How can I bear a son? Since I have not yet known a man but intend to soon enter into relations with Joseph." She would have just presumed that the child would be the son of Joseph.

If Mary and Joseph were part of an ordinary Jewish marriage, she would not be asking about the father of the child. Joseph would be the father of the child, *unless* they were to be celibate in marriage.

Normally, after the espousal the husband would go off and prepare a home for his new bride and then come and receive her into his home where the union would be consummated. This is precisely why Joseph intended to "divorce her quietly" (Mt 1:19) when he later discovered she was pregnant.

This background is significant because a newly married woman would not ask the question "How shall this be?" She would know. Unless, of course, that woman had taken a vow of virginity and the vow was continuing into the marriage.

Mary believed the angel's message in faith, but had no idea how this was going to be accomplished in light of her vow.

This also indicates she was not planning on the normal course of events for her future with Joseph.

Why No Room at the Inn?

Remember how I said I would return to King David's somewhat confusing statement from Psalm 132: "I will not enter my house or get into my bed … until I find a place for the Lord, a dwelling place" for the Ark? Here we go.

There is another strange detail that we take for granted in the Christmas Story. Why was there no room at the inn in Bethlehem for Mary and Joseph?

It was foretold in the Old Testament that there would be no room for Mary and Joseph at the inns of Bethlehem. In addition to Psalm 132, the readings from the Christmas liturgy give us a special insight into the Nativity Story.

The First Reading from Morning Mass on December 24 (Cycle A) comes from 2 Samuel 7:

> When King David was settled in his palace, and the LORD had given him rest from his enemies on every side, he said to Nathan the prophet, **"Here I am living in a house of cedar, while the ark of God dwells in a tent!"** Nathan answered the king, "Go, do whatever you have in mind, for the LORD is with you." But that night the LORD spoke to Nathan and said: "Go, tell my servant David, 'Thus says the LORD: Should you build me a house to dwell in?'"

King David returns home from his victories on the battle-field. These victories were won because David's armies carried the Ark of the Covenant before them into battle. Now David wonders at how the Ark of God dwells in a tent, while he dwells in a palace.

So what do King David's musings have to do with the Christmas story which won't occur for another 1,000 years?

We covered some of David's journeys with the Ark of the Covenant in the last chapter, "What's Really Happening at the Visitation?"

Here, at last, the Ark is done at the end of its long journey. Its journey began at Mount Sinai, where God through Moses first ordered it constructed. The Ark wandered with the Israelites through their forty years in the desert. The Ark crossed the

River Jordan ahead of them and parted the waters, just as before with the Red Sea. The Ark was carried before all of Israel's armies through battle after battle. And now, it has finally arrived in Jerusalem.

So, back to David dwelling in a palace while the Ark of God dwells in a tent. Mary is the New Ark, and where is she forced to dwell? There is no room for Mary and Joseph at the Inn of Bethlehem. The New Ark dwells in a stable. Neither the Old Ark nor the New Ark are permitted a palace, but must dwell outdoors.

Or, the New Ark dwells in a cave to give birth ...

Never fear! The First Reading from December 24, still from 2 Samuel 7, goes on to make a promise:

> The LORD also reveals to you that he will establish a house for you. And when your time comes and you rest with your ancestors, **I will raise up your heir after you, sprung from your loins, and I will make his Kingdom firm.** *I will be a father to him, and he shall be a son to me.* Your house and your Kingdom shall endure forever before me; your throne shall stand firm forever.

The Lord says he will raise up an heir to David "sprung from [his own] loins." But how can this be? King David has been dead from a thousand years when Mary gives birth in Bethlehem. Also, the Lord says that He will be father to the "heir". How can the heir be the child of both King David and God?

Because Christ is born into the family of David. *Mary is a descendant of David,* as the Angel Gabriel confirms at Luke 1:31-33. Also, Christ is the Son of God, confirming both parts of the prophesy. Through the New Ark and Christ, therefore, the throne of David "shall stand firm *forever.*"

The Strange Behavior of the Star of Bethlehem

The Star of Bethlehem does some odd things. The Wise Men are able to follow it until it comes to a rest above Jesus' manger. The star is usually depicted as a tower of light shining down on the nativity scene.

Why is all this happening? We take all this for granted. It's just God doing His thing, right? It's just miracles. Sure, but why this particular combination of miracles?

Here is the description of these events from the second chapter of the Gospel of Matthew:

> When [the Wise Men] had heard the king they went their way; and lo, the star which they had seen in the East **went before them, until it came to rest** over the place where the child was. When they saw the star, they rejoiced exceedingly with great joy.

Why is the light from the star following Mary and Joseph? Do you remember light following anyone else in the Bible?

Remember this image of the *Shekinah*, the "Glory Cloud", from the earlier chapter about the Visitation? It was a tower of light and fire which "overshadowed" the Ark of the Covenant.

The *Shekinah* was a brilliant beacon of light at the center of the Israelite's camp. If the shepherds or their flocks strayed too far from the Israelite camp, the light of the Glory Cloud would lead them back.

The *Shekinah* stayed with Israelites and the Ark of the Covenant for some time, but eventually left them. After the Jews returned from their captivity, a modest Second Temple was completed in 515 BC. But, the visible presence of God as the *Shekinah* cloud of glory did not return.

The *Shekinah* was prophesied to return, however.

The 17th blessing of the daily Amidah (Standing) prayer expresses the longing in the Jewish heart that the *Shekinah* will one day return: "Blessed are You, God, who returns His Presence (Shechinato) to Zion."

So when did the *Shekinah* return? When do we a see a tower of light and fire rising above the Ark of the New Covenant? That is, when do we see a tower of light above the Virgin Mary?

That's right! The Star of Bethlehem.

The light of the star, the tower of light, illuminates the birth of the "light of the world".

We have already discussed how the Gospel of Luke connects Mary to the *Shekinah*. The Holy Spirit "overshadowed" the Virgin Mary when Jesus was conceived in her womb. The word "overshadow" was used in the Old Testament specifically to describe the *Shekinah* Glory Cloud resting above the Ark of the Covenant. Now it rests upon the Ark of the New Covenant, Mary.

But the original *Shekinah* stood as a light to *all* Israel. The conception of Jesus was a private affair. When does the Shekinah shine again for all Israel to see? Even for *all the world* to see?

The *Shekinah* return as the Star of Bethlehem. Look at the star's strange behaviors:

- The star is a tower of light "overshadowing" the Virgin Mary and the entire Holy Family.

- The star is a sign to all Israel, to the shepherds and even to the evil King Herod; and

- The star is visible to the *entire* world! The Magi, the Kings of the East, are guided by the star to Christ's manger.

What does this tell us about Christ and His mission? Christ will bring light to all of Israel and the *entire* world!

Also, as amazing as Moses was, Jesus is far superior. He is God. The Ark of Jesus, too, is far superior to the Ark of Moses. She is a human being. Even Moses' *Shekinah*, as amazing a sight as it was, it is also far exceeded by Jesus' *Shekinah*, the Star of Bethlehem. Moses had a tornado. Jesus had an entire star!

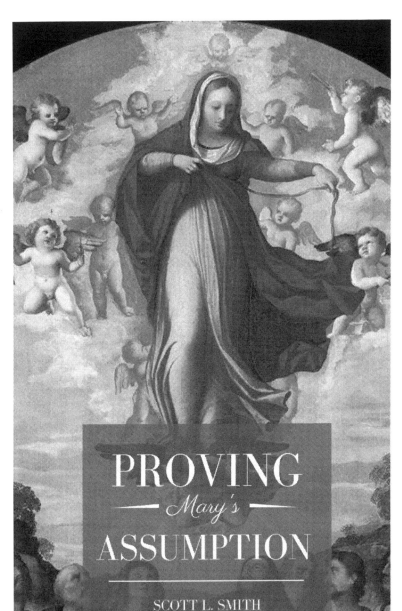

PROVING
Mary's
ASSUMPTION

SCOTT L. SMITH

Chapter 3:
The Assumptions
of Elijah & Enoch

"The Immaculate Mother of God, the ever Virgin Mary, having completed the course of her earthly life, was assumed body and soul into heavenly glory" (Pius XII, *Munificentissimus Deus* 44).

But can we prove this using Scripture? Also, who else was assumed into Heaven according to Scripture? And how do these other assumptions point to Mary?

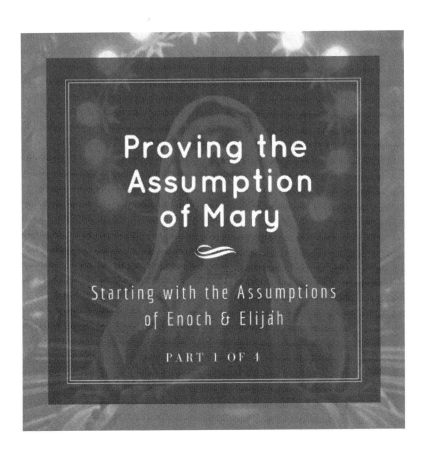

Proving the Assumption of Mary

Starting with the Assumptions of Enoch & Elijah

PART 1 OF 4

Let's start with the obvious: Elijah. Elijah rode his fiery chariot in Heaven at 2 Kings 2:

> And as they still went on and talked, behold, a chariot of fire and horses of fire separated the two of them. And Eli'jah went up by a whirlwind into heaven. And Eli'sha saw it and he cried, "My father, my father! the chariots of Israel and its horsemen!" **And he saw him no more.** (2 Kings 2: 11-12)

This last phrase also points to another assumption, namely, that of Enoch. Enoch's assumption occurs in Genesis 5, where the descendants of Adam are described:

> When Enoch had lived sixty-five years, he became the father of Methu'selah. Enoch walked with God after the birth of Methu'selah three hundred years, and had other sons and daughters. Thus all the days of Enoch were three hundred and sixty-five years. Enoch walked with God; **and he was not,** for God took him. (Genesis 5:21-24)

The two phrases match: "And he saw him no more" & "and he was not."

Figure 5: This is called the Assumption of Enoch and Elijah of Santo Piatti

Some modern Biblical commentators understand the descriptions of these scenes merely as euphemistically describing the deaths of Elijah and Enoch. But ... there's a big problem with that interpretation! This is contradicted by the rest of Scripture (maybe those commentators haven't read the rest of the Bible).

For example, check out the following from the Letter to the Hebrews, chapter 11, where the author is describing faith through the examples of Abel, Enoch, and Noah:

By faith Abel offered to God a more acceptable sacrifice than Cain, through which he received approval as righteous, God bearing witness by accepting his gifts; he died, but through his faith he is still speaking. By faith Enoch was taken up **so that he should not see death**; and he was not found, because God had taken him. Now before he was taken he was attested as having pleased God.

This passage directly refutes the idea that Enoch's death was described in Genesis. It actually says that Enoch was taken up so that he "should not see death."

So there's the New Testament proof that Enoch was assumed into Heaven, but where's Elijah's proof?

Where Do We See Elijah in Heaven in the New Testament?

Or, another question, where do we see Jesus in Heaven in the New Testament and WHO IS WITH HIM?

Figure 6: The upper portion of The Transfiguration by Raphael

The Transfiguration, of course! And who is beside Jesus at the Transfiguration? Elijah and ... Moses. Wait, Moses? Hold onto that thought for a second.

We know that Elijah is in Heaven because *we see him there*! And with Jesus, of all people!

That's not the only time we see Jesus in Heaven in the New Testament? Where else? At Christ's Ascension, right? And again, who do we see beside Christ? Two men. See, for example, Acts of the Apostles, chapter 1 (also Luke 24):

And when he had said this, as they were looking on, he was lifted up, and a cloud took him out of their sight. And while they were gazing into heaven as he went, behold, **two men stood by them in white robes**, and said, "Men of Galilee, why do you stand looking into heaven? This Jesus, who was taken up from you into heaven, will come in the same way as you saw him go into heaven." (Acts 1:9-11)

These two men are in white robes, just like the "dazzling white" of the Transfiguration. [8] To read more on why these two men in white robes are Moses and Elijah (or two angels), check out St. John Chrysostom's homily. [9]

---

[8] Here's a quick textual analysis: (1) the "two men" of Luke 24:4 and Acts 1:10 were dressed in "dazzling white" (*estheti astraptouse*) and "white robes" (*asthesesi leukais*), respectively; (2) Luke mentions "two men" (*andres duo*) who "appeared in glory", namely Moses and Elijah (9:30); (3) Jesus referred to his own resurrected state as "entering into glory" (24:26; cf. 9:32); (4) Jesus' appearance was altered at the Transfiguration, "and his raiment became dazzling white" (*leukos exastrapton*; 9:29, cf. 24:4, Acts 1:10, the "two men"); and (5) Moses and Elijah "spoke of [Jesus'] departure [*exodon,* i.e. "Exodus"], which he was to accomplish at Jerusalem" (9:31).

[9] St. John Chrysostom, Homily 2 on the Acts of the Apostles, Acts 1.6.

Wait – What's Moses Doing in Heaven?

At the Transfiguration, we see Elijah in Heaven beside Jesus and Moses. This is taken as further proof of the Elijah's assumption into Heaven described in 2 Kings 2. But, if this is proof of Elijah's assumption, does that mean Moses, too, was assumed into Heaven? YES!

Chapter 4:
The Assumption of Moses

In Chapter One of this series, we saw the descriptions of Enoch and Elijah's Assumptions in both the New and the Old Testaments. Elijah's Assumption into Heaven is confirmed in the New Testament at the Transfiguration, where we see Moses and Elijah with Christ in Heaven.

The story of Elijah's assumption into Heaven riding on a fiery chariot (2 Kings 2) is well-known, but what about Moses' assumption?

Proving the
Assumption
of Mary

The Assumption of Moses

PART 2 OF 4

But wait! How can it be that Moses was assumed, if Scripture tells us that *he was buried*? Moses' burial is described at Deuteronomy 34:5-6:

> So Moses the servant of the Lord died there in the land of Moab, according to the word of the Lord, and he buried him in the valley in the land of Moab opposite Beth-pe'or; **but no man knows the place of his burial to this day**.

Wait, he was buried, but "no man knows" where? That's a curious statement. The same Israelites who kept the bones of the Patriarch Joseph for hundreds of years and then carried them for another 40 years in the desert (see Exodus 13:19) -- they just lost Moses' bones? Not likely.

How Can Moses be Buried AND in Heaven? The Epistle of St. Jude

Figure 7: The Devil Rebuked (The Burial of Moses) by William Blake

There's a funny little passage in the New Testament in the Epistle of St. Jude:

But when the archangel Michael, contending with the devil, disputed about the body of Moses, he did not presume to pronounce a reviling judgment upon him, but said, "The Lord rebuke you." (Jude 1:9)

What's going on here? Why are St. Michael and the devil disputing over the body of Moses? What's this referring to?

First off, the devil has a claim on Moses' body because is a *murderer.* This occurs at Exodus 2:11-15, where Moses kills an Egyptian who was beating a Hebrew slave.

The Archangel Michael, therefore, is disputing with the devil to reclaim Moses' body for Heaven. This serves, therefore, as one account of how Moses entered into Heaven.

But that's only half of it. St. Jude is citing this episode from *another source.* What other source? The name of the source just happens to be...

The Assumption of Moses, Also Called the Testament of Moses or the Ascension of Moses (*Analepsis Moseos*)

[Interestingly, St. Jude cites elsewhere from another Apocryphal work from another assumptee: Enoch]

The Assumption of Moses is a well-known ancient text. It's not part of the Jewish or Christian canons of Scripture. Instead, it's part of the Jewish Apocrypha. It includes prophesies of the events of the First Century AD. It was likely written around the First Century AD, as well.

A complete copy of the manuscript hasn't survived to the present day, though its existence is testified to by many ancient writers including Origen. Our most complete copy of the work was found in the 1800s inside a 6th century manuscript by Antonio Ceriani in the Biblioteca Ambrosiana in Milan.

So, what does *The Assumption of Moses* tell us about the assumption of Moses?

As I wrote above, several ancient authors wrote about the contents of *The Assumption of Moses*. They describe Joshua seeing **two Moseses** when he was taken up: one with the angels and one honored with burial in the valley.[10] [11] [12]

---

[10] This opinion is shared by Origen, who asserts that in a certain uncanonical book mention is made of two Moses' being seen, one alive in the spirit, the other dead in the body. In Libr. Jesu Nave, Hom, ii. 1: "Denique et in libello quodam, licet in canone non habeatur, mysterii tamen hujus figura describitur. Refertur enim quia duo Moses videbantur, unus vivus in spiritu, alias mortuus in corpore."

[11] Evodius, a contemporary of St. Augustine, has the same gloss, derived from the same source: "When he ascended the mountain to die, the power of his body brought it to pass, that there should be one body to commit to earth, and another to be the companion of his attendant angel." Augustin. Ep. 158 (ii. p. 426, Ben.): "Quamquam et in apocryphis et in secretis ipsius Moysi, quæ, scriptura caret auctoritate, tunc cum ascenderet in montem ut moreretur, vi corporis efficitur ut aliud esset quod terræ mandaretur, aliud quod angelo comitanti sociaretur."

Conclusion

On the one hand, it's clear that Moses is in Heaven from the account of the Transfiguration. On the other hand, it's clear that Moses' assumption into Heaven is an ancient tradition, known to both Jews and Christians.

Nevertheless, we are left with a riddle. How did this all happen and what does it mean? The Mystery of the "Two Moses" will likely remain a mystery -- as well as the ugliest pluralization ever -- until all things are unveiled.

BUT...It all points to something *very* interesting about Mary's Assumption. Find out what next ...

---

[12] Another legend, traced to the same origin, recounts how at Moses' death a bright cloud so dazzled the eyes of the bystanders that they saw neither when he died nor where he was buried. Caten. in Pent. ap. Fabric. Cod. Pseud. Ephesians 5.T. ii. (p. 121.)

Chapter 5:
The Assumption of the Moses' Ark

Let's recap what we've discussed so far, since, after all, "recapitulation" is what's at work here. In Chapters One and Two, we discussed the following:

(1) Elijah was assumed into Heaven on a "fiery chariot", as described in 2 Kings 2:11-12. Elijah's presence in Heaven is confirmed in the New Testament when Elijah stands next to Jesus at the Transfiguration, cf. Luke 9:28-36.

Proving the
Assumption
of Mary

The Assumption of
the Ark of Moses

PART 3 OF 4

(2) Enoch was assumed into Heaven, as described in Genesis 5: 21-24. Enoch's assumption into Heaven is then confirmed in the New Testament in Hebrews 11:5.

(3) Moses' death and burial are described at Deuteronomy 34:5-6. Yet, Moses' presence in Heaven is described in the New Testament when he and Elijah stand next to Jesus at the Trans-

figuration, cf. Luke 9:28-36. Moreover, Moses' assumption is later referred to at Jude 1:9, which itself cites the ancient apocryphal text, *The Assumption of Moses*, whose title speaks for itself.

So, who else, besides the Blessed Mother, was assumed into Heaven? The answer is not *who*, but *what*.

The Ark of the Covenant

First off, what does the Old Testament tell us about the final resting place of the Ark of the Covenant? You will likely need to forget everything you learned watching *Indiana Jones and the Raiders of the Lost Ark*. Well, almost everything, the Ark *was* lost, but it is definitely *not* labeled #9906753 and stored in a wooden crate in some anonymous U.S. government facility.

Second Maccabees, the last book of the Catholic Old Testament, records the following about the Prophet Jeremiah and the Ark of the Covenant:

> It was also in the writing that the prophet, having received an oracle, ordered that the tent and the ark should follow with him, and that he went out to the mountain where Moses had gone up and had seen the inheritance of God. And Jeremiah came and found a cave, and he brought there the tent and the ark and the altar of incense, and he sealed up the entrance. Some of those who followed him came up to mark the way, but could not find it. When Jeremiah learned of it, he rebuked them and declared: **"The place shall be unknown until God gathers his people together again and shows his mercy.** And then the Lord will disclose these things, and the glory of the Lord and the cloud will appear, as they were shown in the case

of Moses, and as Solomon asked that the place should be **specially consecrated.** (2 Maccabees 2:4-8)

So you're probably asking, when does God gather his people again and "show his mercy"? Well, there's Luke 1:46-55, Mary's *Magnificat*, but hold off on that for now.

The Messiah Who Gathers Together the People of God

The ten northern tribes, called the kingdom of "Israel", were scattered in the Assyrian exile in 722 B.C. The two southern tribes, called the kingdom of "Judah" but also including Benjamin, were exiled and the Temple in Jerusalem was destroyed in 587 B.C. Although the two southern tribes returned from exile in 539 B.C., the "lost tribes of Israel" remained scattered among the Gentile nations. This accounted for the so-called diaspora of the Jews. According to the prophets, however, God would one day bring these scattered tribes back to the Promised Land and restore the kingdom of David.

All the Prophets foretold that the Messiah would "gather" together God's people. This is the ingathering of the Twelve Tribes of Israel. Here are just a few examples:

He will raise an ensign for the nations,

and will assemble the outcasts of Israel,
and gather the dispersed of Judah
from the four corners of the earth. (Isaiah 11:12)

I will be found by you, says the Lord, and I will restore your fortunes and gather you from all the nations and all the places where I have driven you, says the Lord, and I will bring you back to the place from which I sent you into exile. (Jeremiah 29:14)

But if we want to find the moment when God "gathers his people" and "shows his mercy", we just need to find the moment when the Ark reappears, right? When do we next see the Ark of the Covenant?

Where Does the Ark of the Covenant Appear in the New Testament?

The Ark of the Covenant appears after the blowing of the Seventh Trumpet at Revelation 11:15-19:

> Then the seventh angel blew his trumpet, and there were loud voices in heaven, saying, "The kingdom of the world has become the kingdom of our Lord and of his Christ, and he shall reign for ever and ever." And the twenty-four elders who sit on their thrones before God fell on their faces and worshiped God, saying,

> "We give thanks to thee, Lord God Almighty, who art and who wast, that thou hast taken thy great power and begun to reign. The nations raged, but thy wrath came, and the time for the dead to be judged, for rewarding thy servants, the prophets and saints, and those who fear thy name, both small and great, and for destroying the destroyers of the earth."

> Then God's temple in heaven was opened, and **the ark of his covenant was seen within his temple**; and there were flashes of lightning, loud noises, peals of thunder, an earthquake, and heavy hail.

In the verses above, all the kingdoms of the world have become the kingdom of our Lord. This is the final gathering of all the people. This is also the time of the Final Judgment when

God shows His mercy. These two things occur and what happens? The Ark of the Covenant is finally seen again.

This is where it gets *really* interesting. Look at the next verse:

> And a great portent appeared in heaven, a woman clothed with the sun, with the moon under her feet, and on her head a crown of twelve stars; she was with child and she cried out in her pangs of birth, in anguish for delivery. (Revelation 12:1)

Wait? The Ark is a ... Woman?

The answer to this last and most amazing riddle of all is the subject of the last chapter.

Chapter 6: The Assumption of Jesus' Ark

This is the final part of this series about the assumptions of the Bible, and how they all, ultimately, point to Christ and the Blessed Mother. We've covered the assumptions of Enoch and Elijah, of Moses and the Ark of the Covenant, and now of the New Moses and the Ark of the New Covenant.

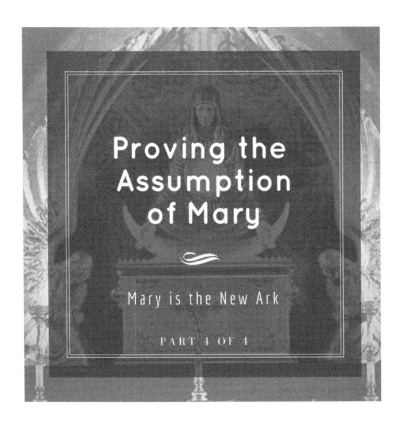

**Proving the
Assumption
of Mary**

Mary is the New Ark

PART 4 OF 4

Here's a summary of the previous three chapters:

(1) Elijah was assumed into Heaven on a "fiery chariot", as described in 2 Kings 2:11-12. Elijah's presence in Heaven is confirmed in the New Testament when Elijah stands next to Jesus at the Transfiguration, cf. Luke 9:28-36.

(2) Enoch was assumed into Heaven, as described in Genesis 5: 21-24. Enoch's assumption into Heaven is then confirmed in the New Testament in Hebrews 11:5.

(3) Moses' death and burial are described at Deuteronomy 34:5-6. Yet, Moses' presence in Heaven is described in the New Testament when he and Elijah stand next to Jesus at the Transfiguration, cf. Luke 9:28-36. Moreover, Moses' assumption is later referred to at Jude 1:9, which itself cites the ancient apocryphal text, *The Assumption of Moses*, whose title speaks for itself.

(4) The hiding of the Ark of the Covenant by the Prophet Jeremiah and its later disappearance is described at (2 Maccabees 2:4-8). Jeremiah also prophesies its return, which occurs at Revelation 11:15-19 ... But it's the next verse where things get really interesting, Revelation 12:1.

Revelation: The Ark is a Woman

It's the triumphant moment of Revelation: the seventh trumpet blast. The long-awaited Ark is about to appear, and this is how it plays out, Revelation 11:19-12:1,

> Then God's temple in heaven was opened, and **the ark of his covenant was seen** within his temple; and there were flashes of lightning, loud noises, peals of thunder, an earthquake, and heavy hail.

> And a great portent appeared in heaven, **a woman** clothed with the sun, with the moon under her feet, and on her head a crown of twelve stars; she was with child and she cried out in her pangs of birth, in anguish for delivery.

Figure 8: "Our Lady of the Sign-Ark of Mercy" St. Stanislaus, Chicago

Who is this woman, who is also the Ark? What can we deduce about her just from these passages?

(A) She wears a crown of twelve stars, one each for each of the Twelve Tribes. She represents then the fulfillment of the ingathering of the twelve scattered tribes of Israel prophesied at Jeremiah 29:14 and also stated just a couple verses earlier at Revelation 11:15: "The kingdom of the world has become the kingdom of our Lord and of his Christ, and he shall reign for ever and ever."

(B) She wears this crown in heaven, so she must be the Queen of Heaven. Since the twelve stars represent the tribes of Israel, she must be the Queen of the unified Kingdom of Israel, which was ruled by the Davidic King and a Queen-Mother.

(C) Her child is the Messiah, because we are told a few verses later at Revelation 12:5 that "she brought forth a male child, one who is to rule all the nations with a rod of iron, but her child was caught up to God and to his throne." The "rod of iron" is a reference to the Messiah from Psalm 2:9.

(D) Lastly and most importantly, if the woman is the mother of Jesus, the Messiah and the New David, she must be the Virgin Mary, the Blessed Mother.

Therefore, Mary is depicted in Heaven. Just like Elijah and Moses and Moses' Ark, Mary is described as being in Heaven in the New Testament. The Virgin Mary was assumed like the others. Just as Moses and Moses' Ark were both assumed into Heaven, so, too, Jesus and Jesus' Ark were both taken into Heaven.

Jesus, of course, stands alone as the only one in the group who ascends, i.e. rises by his own power into Heaven, rather than is assumed there. Ultimately, it is by the grace mediated through Christ that all of these assumptees reach Heaven.

The Covenants of the Old Testament: Pairings

Now, take a look at the covenants of the Old Testament, each of which ultimately points towards Christ:

(1) The Covenant with Creation

(2) Adam

(3) Noah

(4) Abraham

(5) Moses

(6) David

(7) The New Covenant with Christ

Something might look strange to you. All these covenants are listed according to their patriarchs, but each one of these should seem incomplete without their covenantal pairing:

(1) Man & Creation

(2) Adam & Eve

(3) Noah & the Ark

(4) Abraham & Sarah

(5) Moses & the Ark of the Covenant

(6) King David & the Queen

(7) Christ & Mary

Is it any wonder then that Mary is called the New Eve, the mother of all Creation, the Queen of Heaven, and the Ark of the New Covenant?

Mary carries in her womb, Christ, through whom all things were created. Because of this, it can be said that Mary carries within her the New Creation. Just as Eve was, physically, the mother of all the living, Mary is the New Eve, the new spiritual mother of all those who live in Christ. She is also, in a very real way, the New Ark of Noah, which bears all life within it. There is so much more that could be said here. All of these covenants point ultimately to Christ, but to Christ *through Mary*.

Other Proofs that Mary is the Ark of the New Covenant

The following is not meant to be an exhaustive description of all the Scriptural proofs for Mary being the New Ark. There is simply too much, even beyond what I've already written, to go over. I'll just hit the high notes:

(1) Compare the contents of the Ark of the Old Covenant to the contents of Mary's womb. The Ark of Moses contained three things: the tablets of the Ten Commandments, an ephor of manna, and Aaron's rod that budded, the symbol of the high priesthood. Likewise, Mary's womb contains Christ, who is the New Law, the Bread from Heaven, and the New High Priest.

(2) Luke draws several parallels between Mary visiting Elizabeth (Luke 1:39-56) and the Ark coming to David (2 Samuel 6). Check out the chapter entitled "What's Really Happening at the Visitation" for all the hidden connections between these two passages.

(3) The term "overshadow" is used by the Angel Gabriel at Luke 1:35 to describe how the Holy Spirit will come to Mary and conceive in her womb. This same term is used to describe the shekinah, the glory-cloud, that rests upon the Ark of the Covenant, cf. Exodus 40:34-35. Check out the chapter entitled "What's Really Happening at the Visitation" for more on this.

(4) The construction of the Ark of the Covenant is described at Exodus 37. The second verse states that Bez'alel overlaid the Ark with "pure gold within and without." This points towards Mary's virginity as well as her Immaculate Conception.

And this is just the beginning! We're really only just scratching the surface. These are very rich areas of Scripture to study.

Virgin Mary, Blessed Mother, Queen of Heaven, and Ark of God, *please pray for us!*

Part Three:
The New Queen

Chapter 1:
The Hidden Throne of Israel & the Blessed Mother

King Solomon had a problem. He had "700 wives, princesses, and 300 concubines" (1 Kings 11:3). When the king has 1000 -- *one thousand* -- women in his life, who rules as the queen? Also, if Jesus is the New King of Israel, who is the New Queen? The Kingdom of Heaven was the restoration and fulfillment of the Kingdom of Israel, so who is the Queen of Heaven?

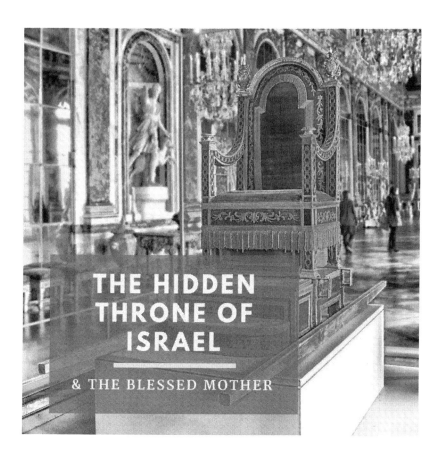

THE HIDDEN
THRONE OF
ISRAEL

& THE BLESSED MOTHER

The answer lies in the following passage from 1 Kings 2. In this passage, Adonijah is asking Bathsheba, the mother of King Solomon, to intercede on his behalf before the king.

The Queen-Mother

But first, some back story: Adonijah and Solomon were both sons of King David. After their elder step-brothers, Amnon and Absalom had died, Adonijah considered himself the heir-apparent to the throne. Adonijah was the oldest living son of David,[13] and therefore had a better claim to succeed King David to the throne. Nevertheless, Solomon fought Adonijah for the throne. Civil War had erupted and Solomon emerged victorious.

First, 1 Kings 2:13-18 RSV-CE:

> Then Adonijah the son of Haggith came to Bathsheba the mother of Solomon. And she said, "Do you come peaceably?" He said, "Peaceably." Then he said, "I have something to say to you." She said, "Say on." He said, "You know that the kingdom was mine, and that all Israel fully expected me to reign; however the kingdom has turned about and become my brother's, for it was his from the Lord. And now **I have one request to make of you**; do

---

[13] Adonijah was actually the fourth son of King David. Altogether, David had about 18 sons according to the various accounts in Chronicles and elsewhere. David's first four sons were Amnon, by Ahinoam; Daniel (also called Chileab), by Abigail; Absalom, by Maachah; and Adonijah, by Haggith. Daniel (or Chileab) is thought to have been dead by the time Adonijah laid claim to the throne. Interestingly, Rabbinic tradition holds that Daniel-Chileab was one of only four ancient Israelites to have died without sin, the others being Benjamin, Amram, and Jesse, the father of King David

not refuse me." She said to him, "**Say on**." And he said, "**Pray ask** King Solomon—**he will not refuse you**—to give me Abishag the Shunammite as my wife." Bathsheba said, "Very well; I will speak for you to the king."

There is some interesting subtext going on in this scene. Notice some of the important parts of this passage:

What does it mean to "pray"?

Adonijah "prays" to Bathsheba, the mother of the King, that she would ask the King to grant Adonijah's "request." This may not be the definition of "pray" we're accustomed to hearing. Adonijah is not "praying" to Bathsheba as if she were God. To "pray" simply means to "ask" or to make a request.

*Question: Do Catholics "Pray" to Mary?

This is really important to remember when you are asked if you "pray" to Mary. "Pray" is being oversimplified here. The question – "Do Catholics pray to Mary" – presupposes a certain, incomplete definition of "pray." Remember how "pray" was used in Shakespeare and Elizabethan era literature? The expressions "pray tell" and "pray come" were used. In *The Taming of the Shrew*, for example, Tranio says, "I pray, sir, tell me, is it possible that love should of a sudden take such hold?"[14] Tranio here is speaking to Lucentio, who is certainly no God. In this sense, do Catholics "pray" to Mary? Yes! We *ask* (pray) for her to pray for us.

What's all this "will not refuse" stuff?

Notice that Adonijah knows that the king "will not refuse" his mother. That sounds like what a good son would do, but why is Adonijah so certain about this?

---

[14] Shakespeare, *The Taming of the Shrew*, Act 1, Scene 1.

In the very next verses, Bathsheba goes to her son, King Solomon, with Adonijah's request (1 Kings 2:19-21):

> So Bathsheba went to King Solomon, to speak to him on behalf of Adonijah. And (1) **the king rose to meet her, and bowed down to her**; then he sat on his throne, and (2) **had a seat brought for the king's mother**; and **she sat on his right**. Then she said, "I have one small request to make of you; do not refuse me." And the king said to her, (3) **"Make your request, my mother; for I will not refuse you."** She said, "Let Ab'ishag the Shu'nammite be given to Adonijah your brother as his wife." [numbers added for explanation]

What an important passage! Several things happened in this second passage that forever affected the structure of the Kingdom of Israel. (1) We see the king "rising to meet" his mother and then "bowing down to her." The king's subjects bow to him. The king bows to no one - except his mother. Before we get to (2), I'll first address (3). The king, himself, reiterates that he "will not refuse" his mother. This is a royal tradition that King Solomon is making a permanent fixture of the kingdom. He is literally about to "enshrine" it.

(2) This is extremely important. The king "had a seat brought for the king's mother" and from then on "she sat on his right". The king placed a seat for his mother beside the throne. King Solomon didn't just have a servant bring a seat for his mother, so she could sit in his court before him. The king

set the seat *beside his own throne*. The mother's chair became a throne in its own right, a royal office subordinate to the king's throne.

This royal office of the Queen-Mother, called the *Gebirah* or the "Great Lady", became a fixture of the King-dom of Israel. It lasted for as long as the Kingdom of Israel lasted. We see in 2 Kings 24, when Judah is at last conquered by the Babylonians and the Southern Kingdom falls to King Nebuchadnezzar, that the Queen-Mother, Nehushta, is still given precedence over the wives of King Jehoiakim (see 2 Kings 24:15). Jeremiah 13:18 also narrates the fall of Israel to the Babylonians in terms of the Queen-Mother losing her crown:

> Say to the king and the queen mother:
> "Take a lowly seat,
> for your beautiful crown
> has come down from your head."

Here the Queen-Mother is depicted as wearing a crown. She is also being given a "lowly seat" – how can this be unless she was first seated at a high seat? Or a perhaps a *throne*?

The tragedy of this verse is finally undone at Revelation 12, where we see that the Queen's crown has been restored and fulfilled, but more on that in a bit. For now, you see from these verses that the Queen-Mother was a constant fixture of the

Kingdom of David and the Kingdom of Israel. If there is going to be a New David and a New Israel, therefore, there must also be a New Queen.

The Queen of Heaven

So, what has this to do with the Virgin Mary? It might be obvious to you by now, maybe not, that the Queen of the Kingdom of Israel was a prefigurement or foreshadowing of the Queen of the Kingdom of Heaven.

How did the kings of Israel, with their many, *many* wives, resolve the issue of who would reign as queen of their kingdom? While a man may have more than wife, every man only ever has one **mother**. The king's mother ruled as queen. This is the tradition of the "Queen-Mother".

This is why we call the Virgin Mary the "Queen of Heaven." This is why we "pray" that Mary will intercede for us before the King, *because that's her royal office.*

If you need more proof that Mary is Queen of Heaven, just read Revelation 12:1, which is discussed throughout this book: "And a great portent appeared in heaven, a woman clothed with the sun, with the moon under her feet, and *on her head a crown of twelve stars.*"

This woman is then described as the mother of the Messiah, i.e. the Virgin Mary. Right there, in black and white, Mary is described as wearing a crown *in Heaven*. Why would Mary be wearing a crown? What is a woman called that wears a crown? A QUEEN, i.e. the Queen of Heaven!

The Wedding at Cana

But there's more ... lots more! Check out the next chapter, "What's Really Happening at the Wedding at Cana," which shows how the scene between Queen Bathsheba and King Solomon is repeated and fulfilled *at the Wedding at Cana!*

Chapter 2:
What's Really Happening at the Wedding at Cana?

There is much, *much* more going on in the Gospel account of the Wedding at Cana than meets the eye. Why does it sound like Jesus is speaking disrespectfully to his mother? Why does Jesus refer to his mother as "woman"? Why does Jesus create wine from *bath water?*

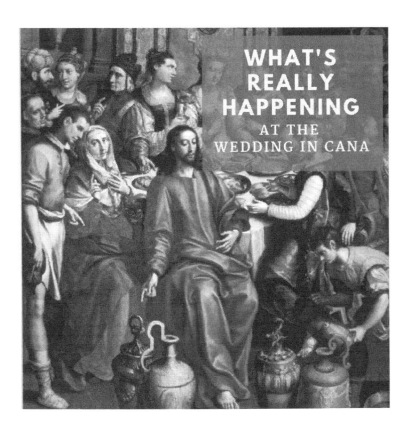

WHAT'S REALLY HAPPENING AT THE WEDDING IN CANA

In the last chapter, the Hidden Throne of Israel, I showed where in Scripture the office of the Queen-Mother of Israel was first established and what this means for the Kingdom of Heaven. You may recall the scene between King Solomon and his mother, Bathsheba, at 1 Kings 2: 13-21. Now, in this chapter, I'll show you where in the Gospels this whole scene is repeated, except with Jesus and *his* mother.

On the 7th Day, There Was a Wedding at Cana

The second chapter of John's Gospel begins "On the third day there was a marriage at Cana in Galilee, and the mother of Jesus was there." In the following verse, John adds "Jesus also was invited to the marriage." Though Jesus is always the center of attention wherever he goes, John is placing special emphasis in this scene on the role of Mary by introducing her first.

Notice the passing of days at the beginning of John's Gospel:

Day 1: "In the beginning ..." (John 1:1)

Day 2: "The next day ..." (John 1:29)

Day 3: "The next day ..." (John 1:35)

Day 4: "The next day ..." (John 1:43)

... then it skips to:

Day 7: "On the third day there was a marriage at Cana in Galilee, and the mother of Jesus was there." (John 2:1)

Why is John setting up this seven-day format for the beginning of his Gospel? It was clearly more than seven days from the beginning of time to the Wedding at Cana, right? Why mention the passing of days if it's not chronological or even logical?

Because there is a *hidden* logic to it! John is setting up the first seven days of the NEW Creation in Jesus Christ. What happened on the seventh day of Creation the first time around? There was a marriage in Eden. Adam and Eve were married: mankind made its first covenant with God.

So who does St. John say is getting married on the 7th day of the New Creation? The newlyweds are unidentified, but who *is* identified? "On the third day there was a marriage at Cana in Galilee, and **the mother of Jesus** was there. **Jesus** also was invited to the marriage." *Jesus and Mary, the New Adam and the New Eve.*

The Queen-Mother is Petitioned/Prayed To

Notice the parallels between the **Wedding of Adoni- jah** from 1 Kings 2 (see the last chapter for more details) and the **Wedding at Cana** from John 2:

> On the third day there was a marriage at Cana in Galilee, and the mother of Jesus was there; Jesus also was invited to the marriage, with his disciples. When the wine failed, the mother of Jesus said to him, "They have no wine." And Jesus said to her, "O woman, what have you to do with me? My hour has not yet come." His mother said to the servants, "Do whatever he tells you." Now six stone jars were standing there, for the Jewish rites of purifica-

tion, each holding twenty or thirty gallons. Jesus said to them, "Fill the jars with water."

In both situations, the king is asked to perform a task he does not want to do and both times his mother is petitioned to intercede before the king. In both situations, the king's mother is petitioned to intercede before the king, and in both, the king "does not refuse" her.

John's Gospel is clearly describing the role of the Queen-Mother in the New Kingdom of Israel by referencing 1 Kings 2.

King Solomon did not want to give Adonijah the bride he was praying for, because with that marriage would come an alliance that would tilt the balance of power against Solomon. Wise King Solomon, therefore, grants Adonijah's request and then kills him.

Jesus, the King of Kings, did not yet want to perform a public miracle, especially one associated with wine because wine would be associated with his "hour" which "has not yet come". Jesus "hour" would be the time of his Crucifixion when he would drink the four cups of wine at Passover, the last of which he would drink on the cross. Nevertheless, like Solomon, he grants his mother's request, creating at least 120 gallons of the finest wine from bath water.[15]

Connection to Baptism

Notice that the jars were filled with water used for Jewish rites of purification, i.e. the Jewish rites from which baptism was born. Jesus, therefore, takes the dirty water left behind from the washing away of our sins and creates exquisite wine.

---

[15] It should be noted that St. John Chrysostom interprets the water as being clean beyond doubt. He states that the jars are described in such a way as to remove all possibility of doubt regarding the miracle, both in terms of their purity, lest anyone think the water merely had the flavor of wine from wine previously stored in the jars (for these jars were "for purification rites" and hence had to be completely clean), and in terms of their volume, that it might be clear that so much water could not possibly be changed to wine except by divine intervention.

Sidenote: Jesus, Not Against Alcohol

Also note - the wedding guests had been drinking *for days*, and Jesus creates for them, on the low side, *six hundred* more bottles of wine! That's a bottle of wine for every one of King

Solomon's wives! After this scene, how could anyone say Jesus is against the drinking of alcohol? There were no little cups of grape juice at this celebration, *just saying.*

Jesus is Not Disrespecting Momma

I have often heard people wonder at Jesus' words to his mother, "O woman, what have you to do with me?" Does this not show that Jesus had cast off his mother? First off, Jesus, even though he was both God and man, would never violate the Fourth Commandment, "honor thy father and thy mother." Even saying that is akin to blasphemy.

So, why then, do Jesus' words sound so harsh? Two things need to be understood: (1) Jesus refers to his mother as "woman" because he is confirming the prophesy of Genesis 3:15 and claiming Mary as the New Eve; and (2) "what have you to do with me" is a phrase indicating the speaker's submission to the will of another.

(1) The New Eve & The Protoevangelium

Remember, the Wedding at Cana occurs on the 7th Day of the New Creation. Just as Adam and Eve were present on the 7th day of the Creation, so the 2nd Adam and the 2nd Eve are present on the 7th day of the New Creation. How is Eve referred to in Genesis? She is called "woman".

Amazingly, though, Mary, too, is also called "woman" in Genesis!

I have written about Genesis 3:15, the *Protoevangelium* or "First Gospel", in the first part of this book, "The New Eve." The idea is that, immediately following the Fall, God tells Adam and Eve, "I will put enmity between [the serpent] and **the woman**." God speaks in future tense, i.e. "I *will* put", so God is speaking of a future woman. In the same verse, God also says the woman's seed will "crush the serpent's head," meaning her child will defeat Satan, i.e. she will be the mother of the Christ. This future woman, the mother of the Messiah, will be an enemy (enmity) of Satan her entire life, even from her conception – her **Immaculate** Conception!

Jesus speaks to this same "woman" at Cana, *the Virgin Mary*, and addresses her as such. This is why Jesus calls Mary, "woman", to show the fulfillment of the prophesy from Genesis -- that Mary is the New Eve!

(2) "What *have* you to do with me?" is the opposite of disrespectful

There is one other time this phrase — "what have you to do with me?" — is used in the New Testament. Do you remember where? It's sort of an unlikely place.

This phrase occurs again in Mark 5. In this passage, Jesus exorcises the Gerasene Demoniac, a possessed man who lived among the tombs and had, several times, broken to pieces the chains which bound him. Here is Mark 5:6-7:

> And when he saw Jesus from afar, he ran and worshiped him; and crying out with a loud voice, he said, "**What have you to do with me**, Jesus, Son of the Most High God? I adjure you by God, do not torment me."

The possessed man "worships" Jesus, saying "what have you to do with me." Though humans might mistake the Son of God for an ordinary man, demons *do not*. Jesus has dominion over the angels, even the fallen ones. After all, He created them. Therefore, they slam themselves to the ground before Jesus and "worship" him. In doing so, the demon directs the same phrase at Jesus that Jesus earlier directed at his mother. "What have you to do with me" does not convey disrespect at all, but quite the opposite. Jesus is conceding to the will of the Queen-Mother.

Conclusion

Can you believe all this meaning is packed into such a short passage? Every Catholic needs to be armed with a thorough understanding of the Wedding at Cana - please share this with friends! Can you see now how important this passage is to the Catholic teaching on the Virgin Mary?

This short Gospel passage is a sweet display of love and affection of a son for his mother. *How grand the gesture!* The King of Kings bowing down to simple peasant girl and placing on her head a "crown of twelve stars." If we are to be like Jesus, we, too, must crown Mary the Queen of our everything.

Chapter 3:
"The Woman" of
Revelation 12

The Blessed Mother also makes an appearance in Revelation 11-12. The Book of Revelation can seem like a very mysterious swirl of apocalyptic images, of angels and monsters. As such, it is very often misinterpreted.

Several sects of Protestantism have become completely consumed by the book. There are the pre-millenialists, the post-millenialists, and every prefix in between. There's the Jehovah Witnesses who proposed to number 144,000 members based on Revelation 7:3-8, until, that is, they grew beyond that number. And, of course, there's the madness centered on the Rapture …

The sad thing is, despite their obsession with the Book of Revelation, many Christian groups completely misunderstand the central figures and the central event of Revelation. In particular, many completely mis-identify "the Woman" of Revelation.

So who is she?

The Return of the Ark

It's *the* triumphant moment of Revelation: the seventh trumpet blast. The long-awaited Ark of the Covenant is about to appear. It had been hidden by Jeremiah on Mount Nebo (2 Maccabees 2:4-8) until, according to the Prophet, "God gathers his people together again and shows his mercy."

So when does God "gather his people" and "show his mercy"? The Messiah was prophesied to gather the Twelve Tribes of Israel back together, as in the time before the breaking apart of the Kingdom of Israel. God will "gather his people" with the restoration of the Kingdom. So first, "thy kingdom come" … comes:

Then the seventh angel blew his trumpet, and there were loud voices in heaven, saying, "The kingdom of the world has become the kingdom of our Lord and of his Christ, and he shall reign for ever and ever." (Revelation 11:15)

The restoration of the Kingdom could perhaps be considered a mercy from God, but the "show[ing] of his mercy" comes with the Last Judgment. This occurs at the very next verse, Revelation 11:16-18:

And the twenty-four elders who sit on their thrones before God fell on their faces and worshiped God, saying,

"We give thanks to thee, Lord God Almighty, who art and who wast, that thou hast taken thy great power and begun to reign. The nations raged, but thy wrath came, and **the time for the dead to be judged, for rewarding thy servants,** the prophets and saints, and those who fear thy name, both small and great, and for destroying the destroyers of the earth."

The dead are judged and the saints are rewarded. The coming of God's kingdom and God's mercy, then, are announced one after another.

So, what's supposed to happen next? Jeremiah said wait for these two things to happen, and then the Ark of the Covenant would re-appear. And that's exactly what happens in the next verses, Revelation 11:19:

Then God's temple in heaven was opened, **and the ark of his covenant was seen within his temple**; and there were flashes of lightning, loud noises, peals of thunder, an earthquake, and heavy hail.

What a flourish! Lightning! Thunder! Earthquakes! Not even a Super Bowl half-time show could compare to the dramatic reappearance of the Ark.

But then, something very strange happens in the very next verse, the Ark is described as a ... what?

And a great portent appeared in heaven, a woman clothed with the sun, with the moon under her feet, and on her head a crown of twelve stars; she was with child and she cried out in her pangs of birth, in anguish for delivery. (Revelation 12:1)

The Ark is described as a ... WOMAN? What? This is a description of the birth of the Messiah, who is Jesus, and his mother, the Virgin Mary.

You might say, but it's two separate appearances, because we just moved from Chapter 11 of Revelation to Chapter 12. Or, maybe it *just seems* to you like two separate, independent heavenly apparitions (SIDENOTE: Isn't it interesting that the first Marian apparition actually occurs in Scripture?).

There are two strong arguments that the appearance of the Ark-Woman is one continuous narrative. First, there were no verse and chapter divisions in the original text. In the original text of Revelation; therefore, there would have been no division between Revelation 11:19 and 12:1. It would just flow one into the other.

Secondly, this is not the first time in Revelation that a sudden switch occurs from one sort of thing, the Ark, to another sort of thing, the Woman. There's another surprising bait-and-switch at Revelation 5.

The Lion of Judah

The re-appearance of the Ark of the Covenant was not the only long-awaited and heavily prophesied event in Jewish history. The coming of the Lion of Judah, the Messiah himself, was also a tremendously important prophesy.

Figure 9: The Appearance of the Lion of Judah in Revelation is the subject of an entire article that I have written. Check my blog for more on this subject.

The prophesy of the Lion of Judah is fulfilled in Revelation 5, when the Lion of Judah appears to break the seal of the scroll, which no one else is found worthy to break:

> And no one in heaven or on earth or under the earth was able to open the scroll or to look into it, and I wept much that no one was found worthy to open the scroll or to look into it. Then one of the elders said to me, "Weep not; lo, **the Lion of the tribe of Judah, the Root of David,** has conquered, so that he can open the scroll and its seven seals." (Rev 5:3-5)

And then, in the very next verse, the most surprising thing happens ... *the Lion disappears!* And something *very different* appears:

> And between the throne and the four living creatures and among the elders, **I saw a Lamb standing, as though it had been slain,** with seven horns and with seven eyes, which are the seven spirits of God sent out into all the earth and he went and took the scroll from the right hand of him who was seated on the throne. (Rev 5:6-7)

Did you catch that? The Lion of Judah is described as a ... what? *A lamb?* The Lion of Judah, the prophesied Messiah that would break the nations with an "iron rod" (cf. Ps. 2:29; Rev 2:27), is just a meek, utterly vulnerable *lamb?* That has been *slain??*

This would be an *astonishing* scene for a Jew in the First Century. The Jews were hungry for a ruler who would overthrow their Roman overlords. They were bristling under the weight of their pagan rulers. Scattered riots and full-blown revolts were breaking out everywhere. Barabbas, whom the people chose to free instead of Jesus (John 18:40), had been a leader of such a riot. Judas Maccabee led a revolt - the subject of the First and Second Book of Maccabees - and established a Jewish kingdom in Judea that lasted a hundred years (164-63 BC) until Rome took over. This was the world Christ was born into. Also, not long after Jesus' death, the outbreak of riots rose to such a fever pitch that the Romans besieged Jerusalem and eventually destroyed the Temple in 69-70 AD.

The destruction of the Temple marked the end of the Jewish religion as it had been known up to that point. The Temple was the political and religious center of Jewish society. Without the Temple, there could be no priests and no sacrifices. From this point on, we see the emergence of Rabbinic Judaism, a form of Judaism based on the texts and not the Temple. Let that sink in ... the destruction of the Temple ended the Jewish priesthood. The Jewish priesthood survived only in the new priesthood established by Christ.

So, imagine this: Fresh from the catastrophic collapse of their religion, the Jews are presented with the *Apocalypse According to Saint John* - what we call the Book of Revelation. Their hopes for the future are ashes until the Lion of Judah enters the scene, ready to break the seal and to conquer. Then, **snap**! Just as quickly as the Lion arrives, he disappears and is replaced by a *Lamb*.

In the exact same way, the re-appearance of the Ark of the Covenant, the box of purest gold, is suddenly and dramatically described as "the Woman."

Chapter 4:
"Hail, Queen of the Jews"?

This is an absolutely critical point in Scripture. First off, if Mary had said "No" to God, it would have changed *everything*. There is so much significance packed into this short verse. The Angel Gabriel says to Mary, "Hail, full of grace, the Lord is with you!" Why does the Angel say, "Hail"? Does the Angel need a taxi cab? And why does the angel say "full of grace" instead of Mary's name?

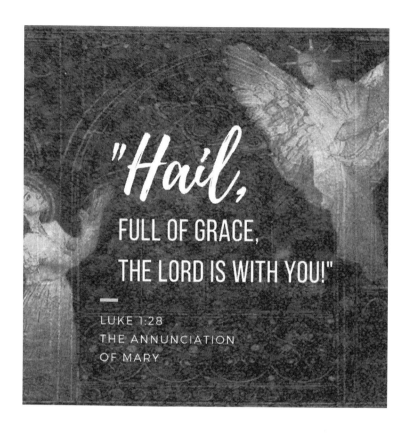

"*Hail,*
FULL OF GRACE,
THE LORD IS WITH YOU!"
—
LUKE 1:28
THE ANNUNCIATION
OF MARY

I was immersed recently in a Twitter battle about the meaning of this verse with some of John MacArthur's[16] hyper-Calvinist disciples. Check it out:

---

[16] John F. MacArthur has been the pastor of Grace Community Church in Sun Valley, California since 1969. MacArthur is a so-called young-earther and a premillennialist. He was also a key figure in the Lordship salvation controversy of the 1980s, in which he and others questioned the once saved, always saved doctrine of many Protestants, taking instead a strong Calvinist line on election. This sort of hardline Calvinism can be summarized by the acronym **TULIP**: (T)otal depravity - mankind is a bomb

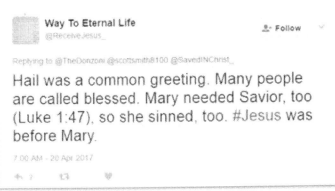

Way To Eternal Life
@ReceiveJesus_

Follow

Replying to @TheDonzoni @scottsmith8100 @SavedINChrist_

Hail was a common greeting. Many people are called blessed. Mary needed Savior, too (Luke 1:47), so she sinned, too. #Jesus was before Mary.

7:00 AM - 20 Apr 2017

Scott
@scottsmith8100

Replying to @ReceiveJesus_ @TheDonzoni @SavedINChrist_

If it's such a common greeting, where else do you see it in the Gospel?

7:04 AM - 20 Apr 2017

crater, nothing good left to it; (U)nconditional election - God chooses some people for eternal life and some for damnation; (L)imited atonement – Jesus only died for the elect, not all mankind; (I)rresistible Grace – even mortal sin cannot impair the working of grace; and (P)reservation of the Saints – once saved, always saved. Lastly, MacArthur is also considered a cessation-ist, one that believes that the gifts of the Spirit, including speaking in tongues, prophecy, and healing, ceased with the Apostolic Age, as opposed to continuationism.

This is a trap, of course. Nowhere in Scripture will you find two Galileans passing each other on the street and saying, "Hail, buddy!"

If you look it up, the word "hail" is actually used only six times in the Gospels. It's used as a greeting (not a weather phenomenon), but what sort of greeting? As you will see, each time, "hail" is used as a very *uncommon* sort of greeting.

(Not sure why he used "norepinephrine" there. It's a pretty ironic auto-correct, though.)

Three of the six times that "hail" is used in the Gospel (Mt 27:29; Mk 15:18; Jn 19:3) it is used as follows:

"Hail, King of the Jews!" (Mk 15:18)

BOOM! Isn't that amazing? "Hail" is used, albeit mocking-ly, to revere and address the "King of the Jews." "Hail" is also followed, not by Jesus' name, but by his *royal title*, King of the Jews. In the exact same manner, Mary is addressed by the angel as "Hail, Full of Grace!" It is a greeting for royalty and "Full of Grace" (Hb. *kecharitomene*) is Mary's royal title.

Also, at Matthew 26:49, Judas greets Jesus with "Hail, Master!" Hail is always used to denote authority and, in particu-lar, *royal* authority.

The John MacArthur boys brought to my attention the sixth time the word "hail" is used in Scripture:

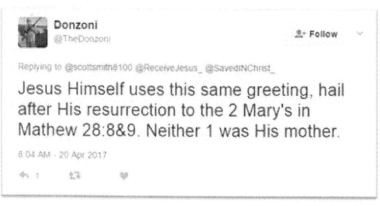

Donzoni
@TheDonzoni

🔲 Follow

Replying to @scottsmith8100 @ReceiveJesus_ @SavedINChrist_

Jesus Himself uses this same greeting, hail after His resurrection to the 2 Mary's in Mathew 28:8&9. Neither 1 was His mother.

8:04 AM - 20 Apr 2017

Scott
@scottsmith8100

Replying to @TheDonzoni @ReceiveJesus_ @SavedINChrist_

Except that right after Jesus said "Hail!", they "took hold of us feet and worshiped him" - Jesus was commanding them to "hail" him.

8:09 AM - 20 Apr 2017

Mary Magdalene and "the other Mary"[17] have found the tomb of Jesus empty. Both Marys had been at the Cross with Mary, the mother of Jesus, and now they have come to Jesus' tomb. They encounter the angel, who announces the Resurrec-

---

[17] Mary of Clopas is mentioned by name only at John 19:25, "Now there stood by the cross of Jesus His mother, and His mother's sister, Mary [the wife] of Clopas, and Mary Magdalene." It would make sense for Mary of Clopas to be the one who accompanies Mary Magdalene to the tomb, as they were together just a few days prior at the Crucifixion.

tion. After departing from the angel, at Mathew 28:9, Jesus meets the women and says, "Hail!" Immediately, they turn and respond, "Howdy, J-sizzle!" ... NO! They do *not.*

Immediately, the women "took hold of his feet and worshiped him."

If Jesus had just said "hello, howdy" to the women, why do they throw themselves at his feet and worship him? Because, when Jesus said "Hail", it wasn't just a mere greeting. He was commanding them to worship him. His resurrected body was wreathed with the glory of God, not unlike at the Transfiguration. It was only fitting that they bow before the revealed power and glory of God. Not to mention, such an apotheosis could be *blinding!* Moses even wore a veil after speaking with God, because his shining face was frightening to the Israelites (Exodus 34:29-35) - just imagine what Jesus' face must have looked like!

Jesus, therefore, uses "Hail!" as a command to bow down and worship. This is an interesting scene with the women bowing down and "hailing" the risen King of Jews. It is perfectly symmetrical with the guards bowing down and mock-hailing Jesus prior to the Crucifixion. See the side-by-side images below:

Figure 10: The Symmetrical Hailings: Ivan Kramskoi "Their Derision Hail King of the Jews" (c. 1870s)

To summarize, *every* time "Hail!" is used in the Gospels, it is used to address royalty and *only* royalty. It is followed by the royal title. For Jesus, it is "King of the Jews. For Mary, it is "Full of Grace." Coming from the angel of heaven, "Full of Grace" is not only Mary's royal title, but her *heavenly* title. We also know from Revelation 12 that Mary wears a crown in heaven and, accordingly, reigns as Queen of Heaven. For more on the Queen of Revelation 12, check out Chapter 4 of "Proving Mary's Assumption."

Mary doesn't just wear any crown at Revelation 12; she wears a crown of "twelve stars," representing the twelve tribes of Israel.

Therefore, the Angel Gabriel could have also said, "Hail, Queen of Israel" ... or **"Hail, Queen of the Jews!"**

Because "a sword will pierce through [Mary's] soul, also" (Luke 2:35).

Chapter 5:
"Hail, Queen of the Muslims"?

Did you know that Muslims also venerate Mary? That they, too, believe in the Immaculate Conception? Most amazing of all, it was no coincidence that Mary appeared at Fatima in Portugal.

What if the 100th Anniversary of the appearance of Our Lady of Fatima marked the beginning of a change in Christian-Muslim relations?

What if it marked the turn of tide in conversions to Christianity?

Find out how all this might be possible as we go through the following topics:

- The difficulty in converting from Islam to Christianity
- The remarkable treatment of the Virgin Mary in the Quran and by Mohammed
- How Fatima, Portugal received its name
- The surprising top destinations of Muslim pilgrimages

The Heresy That Never Declined

Hilaire Belloc, the Anglo-French writer and historian, described Islam as a heresy. If this is true, Venerable Fulton Sheen writes, Islam is "the only heresy that has never declined."[18] Sheen continues that:

> [Other heresies] have had a moment of vigor, then gone into doctrinal decay at the death of the leader, and finally evaporated in a vague social movement. Islam, on the contrary, has only had its first phase. There was never a time in which it declined, either in numbers, or in the devotion of its followers.

We should definitely take note of this, especially given the decline of Christianity in Western Europe. Christianity's attempts to convert Muslims -- even Saints Francis of Assisi and Ignatius of Loyola were stymied in their attempts -- must be largely considered failures. Why might this be?

Here's part of the reason. A Muslim converting to Christianity, at least from the Muslim's point of view, would be much like a Christian converting to Judaism. Muslims believe that

---

[18] Sheen, Fulton, *The World's First Love*, McGraw-Hill Book Co., Inc., New York (1952): 205-6.

they have the final and definitive revelation of God to the world, that Jesus was only a prophet announcing Mohammed, the last of God's real prophets. Though becoming Christian might seem like a step backward for them, Mohammed is merely a prophet of Allah and not Allah, himself. Jesus, however, is both God and man. Therefore, Islam is, in effect, a step backward from Jesus to John the Baptist, the last of the prophets.

Fulton Sheen firmly believes Islam will eventually be converted, but it will not be through the work of missionaries or the direct teaching of Christianity. It will be "through a summoning of the [Muslims] to a veneration of the Mother of God."

The Quran & the Virgin Mary

Mary holds an exalted place in Islam as the only woman named in the entire Quran.[19] It refers to Mary seventy times and even names her as the greatest of all women.

Though rejected by many Protestants, especially those descended from John Calvin, Marian doctrines such as her Immaculate Conception, Perpetual Virginity, and Assumption[20] are wholeheartedly endorsed by the Quran. The nineteenth chapter of the Quran alone contains forty-one verses on Jesus and Mary. It makes such a robust defense of Mary's virginity here that in the fourth book of the Quran, the condemnation of the Jews is attributed to their calumny against the Virgin Mary.

Specific passages and details included in the Quran hint that Mohammed's source text might have been the apocryphal Gospel of Mary's birth. Both texts described the old age and sterility of Saint Anne, while Saint Anne is not even mentioned in the Bible. The Quran even quotes Saint Anne as saying, upon the Immaculate Conception: "O Lord, I vow and I conse-

---

[19] The Quran (sometimes spelled Koran) is the bible of Islam.

[20] Lings, Martin, *Muhammad: His Life Based on the Earliest Sources*, Inner Traditions (rev. ed. October 6, 2006, orig. 1983), p. 101; an example of an Islamic scholar which accepts the Assumption of Mary as an historical fact.

crate to you what is already within me. Accept it from me." And further, upon the birth of Mary, Saint Anne exclaims, "And I consecrate her with all of her posterity under thy protection, O Lord against Satan!" This appears to be a reference to Genesis 3:15, in which God prophesies that a woman will come who will be, from her beginning, an enemy of Satan.

When Saint Joseph asks Mary how Jesus was conceived without a father, this is how Mary answered:

> Do you not know that God, when He created the wheat had no need of seed, and that God by His Power made the trees grow without the help of rain? All that God had to do was to say. 'So be it, and it was done.

The Sayyida

The Quran also describes the Annunciation, the Visitation, and the Nativity. Angels are depicted as addressing the Blessed Mother and saying:

O Mary, God has chosen you, and purified you; He has chosen you above all the women of creation. (Quran 3:42)[21]

Above *all* the women of the earth! This is similar to Elizabeth's address of Mary, "blessed are you among women and blessed is the fruit of your womb." It also reinforces (and in effect *proves*) Mary's own statement: "All generations will call me blessed." When Mary said "all generations," isn't it amazing that her statement should extend beyond Christianity? To *two* world religions?

To the Muslims, the Blessed Mother is the true *Sayyida*, or Lady. The only serious rivals to Mary would be Mohammed's daughter, Fatima, and his wife, both of whom are numbered along with Mary as the four greatest women in Islamic history – interestingly, Mohammed's mother is not on this list.

---

[21] cf. trans. Arberry and Pickthall; Stowasser, Barbara Freyer, "Mary", in *Encyclopaedia of the Qur'ān,* General Editor: Jane Dammen McAuliffe, Georgetown University, Washington DC.

Nevertheless, after the death of Fatima, Mohammed wrote, "Thou shalt be the most blessed of all the women in Paradise, after Mary."[22] Fatima, herself, is even known to have said, "I surpass all women, except Mary."

Sayyida is not the Blessed Mother's only title in Islam. She also bears the titles *Qānitah*[23] and *Siddiqah*. Twice in the Quran Mary is called *Siddiqah,* which means "She who confirms the truth" or "She who has faith."[24]

At least two more Marian titles derive from the beautiful gesture of prayer. These are *Rāki'ah,* which means "She who bows down to God in worship", and *Sājidah*, "She who prostrates to Allaah (God Almighty) in worship." The Quran states: "O Mary, you shall submit to your Lord, and prostrate and bow down with those who bow down."[25] According to some Islamic scholars, Ruku' (bowing down) in Salaah (Muslim prayer) during prayer has been derived from Mary's practice. In this motion, the hands, knees and the forehead of the worshipper touch the ground together. This is the humblest position

---

[22] Sheen, 208.

[23] Mary is called this in sura 66:12. The Arabic term means constant submission to God and absorption in prayer. These meanings coincide with Mary spending her childhood in the temple of prayer. This is likely based on a reference to apocryphal texts, but it is amazing how it supports her being the New Ark in the Temple of God.

[24] Sura 5 (Al-Ma'ida), ayat 73–75 and 66:12

[25] Quran 3.43

one can be in before his Lord, the sincerest sign of humility and surrender to the Creator.

Isn't that amazing? The very posture of prayer and supplication, which so defines our conception of Muslims, is actually derived from the Virgin Mary!

Certain of Mary's titles emphasis the purity of Mary from sin including *Tāhirah* ("She who was purified"), *Sa'imah* ("She who fasts"), and *Mustafia* ("She who was chosen"). Some Muslim traditions record that Mary *Sa'imah* fasted for half a year. The journalist Samir Khalil Samir records the following concerning devotion to Mary *Sa'imah*:[26]

> When I was in Morocco, I found that many women, during pregnancy and after childbirth, continued the so-called "fast of Our Lady," inspired by the Koran, which speaks of this fast.

With regard to the title *Mustafia*, the Quran records the angels as singing: "O Mary! Lo! Allah hath chosen thee and made thee pure, and hath preferred thee above (all) the women of creation."[27] It makes you wonder why Allah preferred Mary above all other mothers, even Mohammed's.

Why Did Our Lady Come to "Fatima"?

---

[26] Samir, Samir Khalil, "Millions of Muslims devoted to Our Lady and eager for exorcism," July 26, 2013: http://www.asianews.it/news-en/Millions-of-Muslims-devoted-to-Our-Lady-and-eager-for-exorcism-28577.html

[27] Quran 3.42

This brings us to a very important question: why the Blessed Mother should have revealed herself in 1917 in the insignificant little village of Fatima, so that to all future generations she would be known as "Our Lady of Fatima"? As discussed above, Fatima was the highly esteemed daughter of Mohammed, who said of herself, "I surpass all women, except Mary."

Fulton Sheen answers the question this way:

> Since nothing ever happens out of heaven except with a finesse of all details, I believe that the Blessed Virgin chose to be known as "Our Lady of Fatima" as a pledge and a sign of hope to the Moslem people, and as an assurance that they, who show her so much respect, will one day accept her Divine Son, too.

Sheen cites the auspicious history of the village of Fatima as evidence for Mary's "pledge".

Muslims, specifically the Moors, had occupied the Iberian peninsula of Portugal and Spain for centuries. The Umayyad Caliphate completed its conquest of Iberia in AD 711. Christians began the long slog of reconquering the peninsula with the Battle of Covadonga in 718 and would not retake their lands for another 700 years, when Ferdinand and Isabella completed the Reconquista in 1492, the year of Columbus.

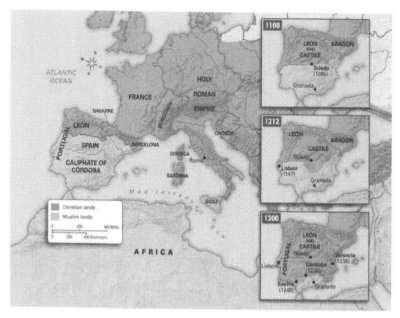

Figure 11: Stages of the Reconquista

At the time when the Muslims were finally driven out of Portugal, the last Moslem chief had a beautiful daughter by the name of Fatima. The story of how the village of Fatima received its name is retold by Friar Bernardino de Brito in his *Chronicle of the Order of Cister* (1602):

> In a surprise attack on Saint John's Day in 1158, a Christian knight, Gonçalo Hermigues and his companions kidnapped a Moorish princess with the famous Arab name of Fatima. The knight took Fatima to a small village of the recently created Kingdom of Portugal, in the Serra de Aire

hills. The princess fell in love with the Christian knight and decided to become herself a Catholic, taking the name of Oureana.[28]

The young husband was so much in love with his wife that he changed the name of the town where he lived to Fatima. Thus, the very place where Our Lady appeared in 1917 bears a historical connection to Fatima, the daughter of Mohammed.

The Blessed Mother & Muslims Today

For further evidence of Mary's purpose in choosing Fatima, one need look no further than the faces of the pilgrims to Fatima, themselves.

Samir Khalil Samir writes for the Asian News Agency PIME about the pilgrims visiting Our Lady of Fatima and other Marian holy sites:[29]

> For years now plane loads of Muslim women from Iran have been landing at Fatima, Portugal. They come to pray before Our Lady who appeared to three shepherd chil-

---

[28] Following her marriage, the princess received as prize the town which she called Ourém, after her name. Ourém remains the name of the municipality which contains the cities of both Ourém and Fatima.

[29] Samir, Samir, "Millions of Muslims devoted to Our Lady and eager for exorcism," July 26, 2013: http://www.asianews.it/news-en/Millions-of-Muslims-devoted-to-Our-Lady-and-eager-for-exorcism-28577.html

dren. The reason is that the Madonna was named after the daughter of Muhammad and wife of Ali Ibn Abi Talib.

Samir also writes about Muslim families flocking to other Marian shrines, especially that of Our Lady of Lebanon:

> In Harissa, Lebanon, Iranian women constantly come to pray to Our Lady, to the point that the rector of the shrine has a chapel prepared especially for them, with icons, signs and prayers to the Virgin in Persian, to facilitate their devotion.

> Last year, during the month of May, as I waited for evening Mass to begin in Harissa, I saw hundreds of Muslim families - probably Shiite - who stopped to listen to the hymns before Mass and who only left at the end.

Popular devotion to these appearances of Our Lady, as well as to Saint Charbel Makhlouf of Lebanon, is growing among Muslims, much to the chagrin of radical Islamists. This is why ISIS and groups such as these destroy pilgrimage sites whenever possible.

About the Author

Scott Smith is an author, attorney, and theologian from Louisiana. Scott is a lover of all things Catholic: the Eucharist, the Blessed Mother, and especially the King of Kings, Who is the hidden connection between all history, Scripture, culture, and theology.

Check out more of his writing and courses below ...

More from Scott Smith

Scott regularly contributes to his blog, The Scott Smith Blog at www.thescottsmithblog.com, WINNER of the 2018-2019 Fisher's Net Award for Best Catholic Blog:

Scott's other books can be found at his publisher's, Holy Water Books, website, holywaterbooks.com, as well as on Amazon

His other books on theology and the Catholic faith include *The Catholic ManBook*, *Everything You Need to Know About Mary But Were Never Taught*, and *Blessed is He Who …* (Biographies of Blesseds). More on these below …

His fiction includes *The Seventh Word*, a pro-life horror novel, and the *Cajun Zombie Chronicles*, the Catholic version of the zombie apocalypse.

ALL SAINTS UNIVERSITY

EST. MMXVII

Scott has also produced courses on the Blessed Mother and Scripture for All Saints University.

Learn about the Blessed Mary from anywhere and learn to defend your mother! It includes over six hours of video plus a free copy of the next book ... Enroll Now!

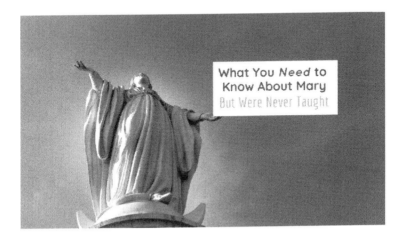

What You *Need* to Know About Mary
But Were Never Taught

What You Need to Know About Mary But Were Never Taught

Give a robust defense of the Blessed Mother using Scripture. Now, more than ever, every Catholic needs to learn how to defend their mother, the Blessed Mother. Because now, more than ever, the family is under attack and needs its Mother.

Discover the love story, hidden within the whole of Scripture, of the Father for his daughter, the Holy Spirit for his spouse, and the Son for his MOTHER.

This collection of essays and the All Saints University course made to accompany it will demonstrate through Scripture how the Immaculate Conception of Mary was prophesied in Genesis.

It will also show how the Virgin Mary is the New Eve, the New Ark, and the New Queen of Israel.

Catholic Nerds Podcast

As you might have noticed, Scott is obviously well-credentialed as a nerd. Check out Scott's podcast: the Catholic Nerds Podcast on iTunes, Podbean, Google Play, and wherever good podcasts are found!

The Catholic ManBook

Do you want to reach Catholic Man LEVEL: EXPERT? *The Catholic ManBook* is your handbook to achieving Sainthood, manly Sainthood. Find the following resources inside, plus many others:

- Top Catholic Apps, Websites, and Blogs
- Everything you need to pray the Rosary
- The Most Effective Daily Prayers & Novenas, including the Emergency Novena
- Going to Confession and Eucharistic Adoration like a boss!
- Mastering the Catholic Liturgical Calendar

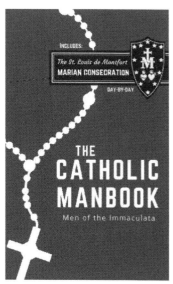

The Catholic ManBook contains the collective wisdom of The Men of the Immaculata, of saints, priests and laymen, fathers and sons, single and married. Holiness is at your fingertips. Get your copy today.

NEW! This year's edition also includes a revised and updated St. Louis de Montfort Marian consecration. Follow the prayers in a day-by-day format.

Blessed is He Who ...
Models of Catholic Manhood

You are the average of the five people you spend the most time with, so spend more time with the Saints! Here are several men that you need to get to know whatever your age or station in life. These short biographies will give you an insight into how to live better, however you're living.

From Kings to computer nerds, old married couples to single teenagers, these men gave us extraordinary examples of holiness:

- Pier Giorgio Frassati & Carlo Acutis – Here are two extraordinary **young men**, an athlete and a computer nerd, living on either side of the 20th Century
- Two men of royal stock, Francesco II and Archduke Eugen, lived lives of holiness despite all the world conspir-ing against them.
- There's also the **simple husband and father**, Blessed Luigi. Though he wasn't a king, he can help all of us treat the women in our lives as queens.

Blessed Is He Who ... Models of Catholic Manhood explores the lives of six men who found their greatness in Christ and His Bride, the Church. In six succinct chapters, the authors, noted historian Brian J. Costello and theologian and attorney Scott L. Smith, share with you the uncommon lives of exceptional men who will one day be numbered among the Saints of Heaven, men who can bring all of us closer to sainthood.

THANKS FOR READING! TOTUS TUUS

Made in the USA
Middletown, DE
06 June 2024

55439395R00099